D1479485

THE BLUEGRASS OF KENTUCKY
A Glimpse at the Charm of Central Kentucky Architecture

By

Richard S. DeCamp

Photography By

Patricia S. DeCamp

To our friend Walt Barbour
With best wishes,
Richard DeCamp
Patricia DeCamp

December, 1985

The Rayburn Press
Lexington, Kentucky
1985

THE BLUEGRASS OF KENTUCKY
Copyright © 1985 by
Richard S. DeCamp

All rights reserved. No part of this book may be
used or reproduced in any manner whatsoever without
the written permission of the publisher, except in
the case of brief quotations embodied in critical
articles and reviews.

The Rayburn Press
Lexington, Kentucky

Library of Congress Catalog Card Number: 85-63222
ISBN # 0-9615942-0-9

Printed by
The Thoroughbred Press
Lexington, Kentucky

THE BLUEGRASS OF KENTUCKY

CONTENTS

ACKNOWLEDGMENTS

IN PUTTING TOGETHER THE BRIEF INFORMATION ON THESE BLUEGRASS BUILDINGS, I AM indebted to many people who have great interest in our region's architectural heritage and who have been helpful to me in recommending sites and passing on information.

First, the most important people, for it is these three who by their work on architecture and history had a great deal to do with my becoming interested in the field. Architectural historian Clay Lancaster, by his survey work, drawings, and writings, was one of the first to make people aware of the treasure trove of architecture existing in the Bluegrass. His valuable work continues, not only on Kentucky buildings but on a great many architectural styles in many different locations. Bettye Lee Mastin, Lexington newspaperwoman and expert on Kentucky architecture, has spent many productive years studying and writing on this phase of Bluegrass culture. Burton Milward, who has always provided an unending wealth of information on any phase of Central Kentucky history, has been generous and helpful beyond measure.

In Fayette County, I relied heavily on the work of the late Beebe Park. Her superlative survey of Fayette County buildings is a constant reference source. Scott County is fortunate to have Ann Boltin Bevins, whose book *A History of Scott County as Told by Selected Buildings* is a complete and thorough documentation of this architecturally rich county. In Clark County, I had good direction from Mrs. Edward Houlihan, Mrs. Julius Clark, and Miss Kathryn Owen. Miss Owen is the author of *Old Homes and Landmarks of Clark County, Kentucky*. Assistance in Woodford County came from Mrs. Ben Chandler and Mrs. Conrad Feltner. In Jessamine County, I was fortunate to have valuable help from Mrs. Weldon Simpson, who lectures with knowledge and charm on the houses in her county. Bourbon County is fortunate to have had the very competent architectural historian Walter Langsam do a survey of this historically and architecturally rich Bluegrass county, published under the title of *Architectural History of Bourbon County*. Mr. Langsam had the able assistance of Mr. William G. Johnson of the Kentucky Heritage Council in compiling this informative book. Also in Bourbon County, I'm indebted to the late Mrs. Robert Van Meter.

Other important sources must be noted. The late Elizabeth M. Simpson wrote two lovely books in the 1930s that are chatty, charming, and informative and that capture the lore of many Bluegrass houses. The work of architectural historian Patrick Snadon is always a source of important information. Last, but not least, is our state agency, the Kentucky Heritage Council. Its dedicated staff has produced professional architectural and historical survey information, which has been invaluable to this project.

Of course, without the cooperation of the property owners, I never could have started work on this book. My sincere apologies to the many people whose buildings we could not use due to space limitations. There are many architecturally important structures in the Central Kentucky region, and they all contribute to making the Bluegrass area one of the unique places in the world.

—Richard S. DeCamp

FOREWORD

THE ESSENCE OF A TIME, PLACE, AND PEOPLE IS BEST CAPTURED AND PRESERVED IN buildings, whether residential, business, or institutional structures. This is certainly true of the Central Bluegrass area, where the diversity and richness of its architectural achievements provide an invaluable heritage to all who live or visit here.

To appreciate the character and style of life of the Bluegrass gentry who settled and developed this incomparably fertile area, one must see and explore the structures that were built by these notable individuals. Their houses not only reflect the prevailing style of a period, but also bear the hallmarks of the architects and special personalities of the owners.

For anyone wishing to savor the unique quality of Bluegrass life from the late eighteenth century through the nineteenth century, Richard and Patricia DeCamp have prepared a handy, informative, and well-illustrated overview of distinctive houses in the Central Bluegrass.

The way of life of antebellum Kentucky, strongly southern in tone with its large farms, is reflected in the spacious houses that grace this lovely landscape. Here hemp, tobacco, and farm products were raised, and high grade livestock and matchless horses were bred, while slave labor was exploited to cultivate the land, build stone walls, and erect houses. The tradition of hospitality, transferred from Virginia to Kentucky, was bountifully displayed here. Glistening cherry tables were laden with fine food and aged bourbon, and festive dances lasted into the early hours.

The familiar forms of Georgian and Federal architecture were soon embellished with the colonnaded Greek Revival style. Yet there was no deadening uniformity because the strong individuality of the builders created a distinctive architectural style expressed in their buildings.

The rural character of the Bluegrass in the pre–Civil War period accounts for the large majority of these houses being located on farms. Yet the flourishing community of Lexington could boast of impressive townhouses and could lay claim to having in John Wesley Hunt the West's first millionaire. His house, Hopemont, reflects his wealth and lifestyle and is surrounded by a number of fine residences clustered around Gratz Park, an area that strongly evokes the antebellum atmosphere.

Architectural styles had already begun to change by the time of the Civil War as neo-Gothic and Italianate influences affected the architects' outlooks and the builders' preferences. The war inevitably changed the way of life of many Bluegrass residents. Lexington developed into a larger and more urbanized center as it incorporated electrification, telephones, and the street railway into its living pattern. The late Victorian style and a greater eclecticism molded the forms of the newer houses rising on the city's expanding borders.

Yet, in the countryside, despite the impact made on farm life by the elimination of slave labor, migration to the cities, and the ending of the hemp industry, the distinctive Bluegrass mode of living was largely preserved. The aristocratic thoroughbreds grazed leisurely on the white-fenced pastures and the proud mansions surveyed the broad estates as, indeed, they do to this very day. The DeCamps' *The Bluegrass of Kentucky: A Glimpse at the Charm of Central Kentucky Architecture*, provides an attractive view to a fuller appreciation of the unique Bluegrass atmosphere and style, manifested in its splendid architecture.

—John D. Wright, Jr.
Historian & Author

PREFACE

THE HISTORY OF THE BLUEGRASS REGION OF KENTUCKY RECORDS THE EXPLORATION AND settlement of an important part of the lands west of the Allegheny Mountains. It is as colorful a history as any in our country, and today, more than 200 years later, remnants of these early times still can be seen and felt. Nothing offers a more tangible tie to bygone days than the remains of the man-made environment of an area. Many early buildings of architectural worth stand in Central Kentucky as a constant reminder of the settlers who cleared the land, developed the farms and the towns, brought in the blooded livestock, and built the fine buildings. In so doing, they left a legacy that we now have the privilege of glimpsing—perhaps through a grove of trees on a country road or in a quiet residential area or in our bustling commercial centers.

This area of Kentucky was explored in the late 1700s and was described by George Rogers Clark in 1775: "A richer and more beautiful country than this I believe has never been seen in America yet." The news of this beautiful and fertile land traveled rapidly back to the East, and by 1790 the population of Kentucky was over 73,000. While settlers came from North Carolina, Pennsylvania, and Maryland, the majority migrated from Virginia. Because Virginians followed the English tradition of primogeniture, many "second sons" of aristocratic Old Dominion families crossed the Cumberland Gap or came down the Ohio River in hopes of finding a livelihood in this fertile outpost. They brought with them the customs of their cultures, which led to the establishment of estates adorned with fine mansions. Less elegant buildings were more prevalent, constructed first of log or stone and later with locally-fired bricks. Some of these early buildings have survived and today are scattered throughout the Bluegrass region.

In his book *Ante Bellum Houses of the Bluegrass*, noted architectural historian Clay Lancaster describes the building styles in Fayette County which can be applied to the surrounding area as well:

> The houses built in Fayette County during the three-quarters of a century preceding the Civil War fall into several successive categories or periods. The earliest ones are distinguished by the construction materials: rough native logs, shaped timbers, frames, and stone in rubble and ashlar forms. After the introduction of brick as a building substance, houses may be divided according to styles. Lingering medieval characteristics are to be found throughout the first brick phase. This is followed by a period of refinement and originality. Authority from abroad next is sought during the reign of classicism, but the classic or Federal period in Kentucky is not without a

decidedly local twist. Architecture next takes on a more heavy, masculine quality, as the source of inspiration shifts from the effete grandeur of the Romans to the virile simplicity of the Greeks. The Greek Revival, however, was not without its romantic aspect. The undercurrent of romanticism finally emerged and stood boldly exposed in the lacy picturesqueness of the Gothic Revival. Increased wealth and the leisure resulting from it, with its accompanying reveries, plus prosaic technical advances, made possible the opulence of the manors built during the middle decades of the nineteenth century. The irregularity of Gothic massing and restraint of Greek details came together in the Italianate villas that climaxed, and to some extent summarized, much that had preceded them in Bluegrass building. The villas also display an eclecticism foreshadowing what was to predominate architecture in this area following the sterile years of the war.

It is this legacy of the built environment in the Bluegrass that has been of great interest to my wife and me. We have been driving, biking, and walking this area for a number of years and have wanted to share the visual rewards of our ramblings. We selected six counties of the Inner Bluegrass area for documentation, with the greatest emphasis on Fayette County, partly because we are most familiar with it and also because it is the location of Lexington, the major city of the Bluegrass. In addition, we have included five counties contiguous to Fayette that are either fully or partly within the area geologically described as the Inner Bluegrass of Kentucky. These counties are Bourbon, Clark, Woodford, Scott, and Jessamine. Patricia has photographed a representative number of pre-1900 buildings in all of these counties and I have provided the descriptive material.

As we present the results of our architectural ramblings through these counties, we hope that our readers begin to feel that uniqueness that makes the Bluegrass region of Kentucky known the world over. It is also our hope that this focus on its architectural heritage will result in renewed efforts to preserve those remaining structures that we now are so privileged to enjoy.

—Richard S. DeCamp

FAYETTE COUNTY

ROSE HILL

A SIMPLE SHAFT OF BROWN GRANITE FROM MONTROSE, SCOTLAND, MARKS THE GRAVES in a Lexington cemetery of John Brand, "immigrant from Scotland," and his wife Elizabeth Hay. In her book *Bluegrass Houses and Their Traditions*, Elizabeth M. Simpson wrote: "But it is near Fifth Street on Limestone, long ago known as Mulberry Lane, that Rose Hill . . . stands as a lasting monument to those early Scottish settlers in Kentucky."

John Brand was born in Montrose, Scotland. After his business as a manufacturer of sailcloth failed, he fled to France where he met an old friend, Dr. Alexander Humphreys, an eminent professor of surgery at the University of Glasgow. With Humphreys' urging and financial help, Brand and his wife came to America and, after a short stay in Philadelphia, settled in Lexington.

By 1802, Brand and John W. Hunt, later reputed to be Lexington's first millionaires, had established a factory in which they manufactured hemp bagging. Brand prospered and purchased the west side of the block on Limestone Street between Fourth and Fifth Streets. On the south portion of the property he set up a "rope walk," a large shed-type building where hemp fibers were twisted into rope, and on the north end he built the beautiful Rose Hill in 1812.

Brand's financial success allowed him to return to Scotland in 1818 and "settle-up" with his Scottish creditors. The story is that he invited them all to a lavish dinner and there paid his financial obligations. This gesture of honor created comment in the press on both continents, and one story referred to John Brand as "one honest man in America."

This five-bay brick house, flanked by lower wings on either side, is enhanced by its entranceway with elliptical fanlight and wide leaded sidelights with clustered colonnettes. Clay Lancaster in *Ante Bellum Houses of the Bluegrass* says, "The Greek Ionic portico dates from at least a quarter of a century later. . . . The portico adds interest to the entrance and is in perfect harmony with preexisting forms. . . . No house in Kentucky better deserves to be preserved and maintained for its architectural merits."

Rose Hill has changed little over the years in spite of changes in the character of the surrounding area. The present owners have steadfastly maintained this architectural gem for many years, and it is a fitting coincidence that they are descendants of the same Dr. Alexander Humphreys who financed John Brand's migration to America.

Rose Hill

Parlor

THE OLD KEEN PLACE

In the late 1700s, Francis Keen of Fauquier County, Virginia, purchased from Patrick Henry the land on which this historic house was built. The tract amounted to over 6,000 acres. The main block of the house was constructed for Francis Keen in the 1790s, and it remained in that family until 1948.

The night of May 15, 1825, is noteworthy for the Old Keen Place. It was then that Major John Keen and his wife Mary entertained an overnight guest, the Marquis de Lafayette. The joint host was Mary Keen's father, Colonel Abraham Bowman, who had served in the Revolutionary War and was an old friend of Lafayette's. Colonel Bowman had wanted to entertain the marquis at his house, but because of the remoteness of Bowman's farm, it was decided to hold the reception at his daughter's house. According to Elizabeth Simpson in her book *Bluegrass Houses and Their Traditions*, "Lafayette's military escort camped on the grounds during the night, and the following day the marquis, accompanied by Colonel Bowman, drove into the city in a carriage drawn by four bay horses, and was taken to his suite at the Phoenix Hotel, of which Mrs. Sanford Keen was then owner. Lafayette spent forty-eight hours in Fayette County, during which he was feted in many houses, but only under the roofs of the Keens did he spend the nights of the memorable visit."

The main part of the house is a two-story, six-bay section with the façade laid in Flemish bond brick. Over the years, to meet the needs of the different Keen family members, one-story wings were built on to either side of the main block of the house and enlargements were made in the rear wing. It was not until 1925 that the columned portico was added on the front and, presumably, the balustrades on the wings. In spite of changes, much of the original fabric remains, adding historic integrity to this early Bluegrass structure.

It was John Oliver Keene (some members of later generations added an *e* to the name) who began construction of the famous thoroughbred race track and clubhouse, which he sold to the Keeneland Association in 1935. Every year, many thousands of visitors to Keeneland Race Course catch a glimpse of the Old Keen Place, situated on a gentle knoll approached through a tranquil setting of trees.

Horse racing is a tradition in Lexington going back to the days of Francis Keen. The other great tradition, Kentucky hospitality, was lavishly displayed during the famous visit of the Marquis de Lafayette when he was honored by the Bowmans, the Keens, and other gentry of the Bluegrass.

The Old Keen Place

LOUDOUN

PERHAPS THE FINEST GOTHIC REVIVAL HOUSE IN THE SOUTH, LOUDOUN WAS constructed in 1849–50 for Francis Key Hunt on the northeast edge of Lexington. Hunt went to A. J. Davis of New York, one of the best-known architects of that period, to design his house, and had John McMurtry, Lexington's well-known architect-builder, erect Loudoun from Davis' plans at a cost of over $30,000, making it probably the most expensive house here at the time.

Davis is credited with many of the house plans in popular nineteenth-century-pattern books and designed some of the fabulous houses in the Hudson River Valley. He designed for Mr. Hunt a romantic mansion, for Loudoun is castle-like with towers, turrets, oriel windows, and buttresses. The walls are of hollow brick construction which provides an air space for insulation. The outer walls were originally covered with paint mixed with sand to give them a texture similar to stone.

Francis Key Hunt was a prominent lawyer and the son of John Wesley Hunt, Lexington's first millionaire. He married Julia Warfield whose father, Dr. Elisha Warfield, had an estate, The Meadows, which adjoined Loudoun. Mr. Hunt died in 1870, and his widow remained at the house until 1884, when she sold it to Colonel William Cassius Goodloe. Goodloe had served his uncle, Cassius Marcellus Clay, as secretary when Clay was ambassador to Russia, and during the Civil War Goodloe was commissioned assistant adjutant general by President Lincoln. He later served in the General Assembly of Kentucky and was chairman of the national committee of the Republican party. President Hayes appointed him minister to Belgium.

After Goodloe's death, his widow sold the front portion of land for building lots and in 1923 sold the house and the rest of the land. Several years later, the new owners sold the property to the City of Lexington for a recreation center and playground. Today the house serves as headquarters for the Lexington Art League.

Over 130 years after its construction, Loudoun, stripped of the glorious furnishings of former owners, stands among the few remaining stately trees, a reminder of that great romantic period of architecture that had its moment of glory in the Bluegrass.

Loudoun

HURRICANE HALL

According to Clay Lancaster, "The most engaging residence in Fayette County of which a part predates 1800 is Hurricane Hall." The main section is the two-and-a-half-story eighteenth-century portion. In 1805, Roger Quarles, who had come to Kentucky from Spottsylvania County, Virginia, bought the house and 190 acres. Soon after, Quarles added a one-and-a-half-story wing, and his grandson, Patrick Henry Thomson, added the one-story wing in the 1840s. Henry Thomson and his wife Julia Farnsworth had twelve children. It has been said that the many Thomson children ran through the house like a hurricane, resulting in its being called Hurricane Hall. The Quarles-Thomson family lived here for six generations, until it was sold in 1962.

Bettye Lee Mastin, Lexington historian, has written: "Hurricane Hall is rare in Fayette County in that its oldest section has a panel chimney breast, gougework cornices, and window frames with unusual reentrant angles. The dining room and two upstairs rooms retain cupboards of unusual charm." Another elegant feature is the great hall, which one enters through the front door, and this fifteen-foot stairhall serves as an indispensable living area of the house. One of the most appealing decorative features of the house is the scenic parlor wallpaper, which was hung for the 1817 wedding of Eliza Quarles to her cousin William Z. Thomson.

The present owners have rehabilitated the house with meticulous care, along with the schoolhouse (now a guesthouse) and smokehouse. Hurricane Hall also has a fine thoroughbred breeding operation known as Hurricane Stud and is a house that continues the great Kentucky tradition of hospitality.

School House and Smoke House

Hurricane Hall

Parlor

WAVELAND

THOUGH NOT PRETENTIOUS IN DESIGN, WAVELAND IS CONSIDERED ONE OF THE FINEST examples of Greek Revival architecture in Kentucky. The house sits gracefully atop a small knoll surrounded by farmland, and in the distance, the growing metropolis of Lexington can be seen.

Daniel Boone's sister Mary married William Bryant in 1755, and it was for their son and his namesake, Daniel Boone Bryant, that he "laid off" a tract of land south of Lexington. According to the brochure describing the house, Daniel Bryant "built a stone house and surrounded it with a plantation village. His gunsmith shop employed as many as 25 men, he had a gristmill, a distillery, a blacksmith shop and a paper mill on the property as well as a Baptist church and a female seminary. Daniel Bryant's son Joseph razed the stone house, replacing it with the present mansion which was completed in 1847."

In nominating Waveland to the National Register of Historic Places, Dr. Hambleton Tapp wrote, "The house contains some fourteen high-ceiling rooms and spacious hallways. A magnificent tetra-style Ionic portico graces its façade, and the main doorway wears a frieze which is a perfect copy of the north entrance to the Erechtheum on the Athenian Acropolis. The doorway features distyle-in-antis Ionic columns. Pilasters adorn the walls and support a denticulated entablature. The roof is low hip, covered with standing seam metal."

Waveland remained in the Bryant (Bryan) family for several generations. In 1956, the University of Kentucky bought the land to use as an experimental farm, and the following year the state opened the house to the public. Activities abound in this stately building, whose builder was a descendant of two of Kentucky's pioneer families.

Outbuilding

Waveland

Library

Dining Room

13

MALVERN HILL

MALVERN HILL IS LOCATED ON THE EDGE OF LEXINGTON IN AN AREA THAT RECENTLY has been developed commercially. Nevertheless, as one drives through the gates and back beyond the sight of the main road, the cares of the modern-day world disappear as this charming house comes in view.

Built in the 1790s by the Rev. James Moore, it was named Vaucluse after a town in southern France. Moore was a lover of music and a violin player, who was immortalized in James Lane Allen's short story, "Flute and Violin." The high-ceilinged parlor was designed for his beloved musicales. A man of great learning, the Rev. Mr. Moore served as president of Transylvania University and was organizer of Kentucky's first Episcopal Church.

In 1838, the property was purchased by the Redd family. The well-known artist, Oliver Frazer, who had studied under Matthew Jouett and married Martha Bell Mitchell, bought the house from his wife's aunt in 1857. He changed its name to Eothan and lived and painted there until his death in 1864. It stayed in the Redd-Frazer family for over 100 years. One of the last of the family to live there was the colorful Richard Menefee Redd. A veteran of the Civil War, "Colonel Dick" nearly became a professional Confederate, for he was often seen in his full-dress Confederate uniform on his horse Major. He was well known for his "Rebel yell" and for years led almost every parade in Lexington.

The house has seen many changes during the years, but none has detracted from its charm. Originally Georgian in style, it took on elements of Classicism with the addition of a columned porch in 1840. A wing was added in later days. Remaining on the property are an old slavehouse, a nineteenth-century studio, an icehouse, and the milkhouse. Several other buildings have been adapted for other uses.

In 1934, the house was sold, and the new owners changed its name to Malvern Hill. Malvern Hill-Eothan-Vaucluse has had several artistic owners, who were perhaps inspired by this charming Kentucky house and its surrounding gardens.

Malvern Hill

DUNREATH

DUNREATH, SCOTTISH FOR "WOODED HILL," WAS THE HOUSE THAT JOHN HOWARD Sheffer started in 1848 for his bride, Julia Hughes, and completed in 1854.

According to the late author Elizabeth Simpson, John Sheffer came to Lexington from Philadelphia to collect accounts for a wholesale dry goods house. On the road east of Lexington, he met William Rodes Estill, who was here from Mississippi to buy stock for a Southern plantation. As they rode together, they probably talked of business and Kentucky ladies, and as they parted, they agreed to meet again back in Kentucky after their marriages.

Within a few years, Estill married the girl who lived in the house at that point on the road where the two men had met, and Sheffer returned to wed at the house known as Leafland, where the two men had parted company. Eventually two Sheffer daughters married two Estill sons, and in later days an Estill granddaughter married a Sheffer grandson.

Dunreath is Greek Revival in style and is locally referred to as one of the "Winchester Pike" group—several large houses of approximately the same period and in the same general area of the county. According to Clay Lancaster, "Each is composed of a heavy two-storied mass crowned by a low-pitched hipped roof, the façade pierced by triple openings of rather narrow proportions, the center doorway sheltered by a small portico having square piers. Shorter wings of one or two stories are variously attached to the sides."

Several early outbuildings remain in the yardlot of Dunreath. The present owners, who have had the property over the past twenty years, keep it well maintained as a thoroughbred and cattle operation.

Dunreath

LEAFLAND

THIS MID-NINETEENTH-CENTURY GREEK REVIVAL HOUSE WAS ONE OF SEVERAL BUILT IN a similar design during the same period and in the same section of Fayette County. All these houses have hipped roofs, narrow triple windows on the front, center doorways with small one-story porches, and usually a wing or two on either side of the main block. These houses have become known locally as the "Winchester Pike" style.

Leafland was built about 1850 for Jacob Hughes, the son of Colonel Cornelius Hughes, a Revolutionary War veteran who came into Kentucky from Spottsylvania County, Virginia, in 1797. Initially, Colonel Hughes settled on a 2,000-acre government grant in Northern Kentucky but eventually moved to Fayette County. Jacob was described in Perrin's 1882 *History of Fayette County, Kentucky* as "one of the pioneers of Fayette County who acted an important part in subjecting the county to the use of man, and in transforming it into the paradise we find it today."

The setting at Leafland has changed little in the approximately 130 years since it was built. The smokehouse and one early slave house are still standing, but more important, the Graves family members who reside at Leafland are the direct descendants of Colonel Hughes, the frontiersman who was at Yorktown when Cornwallis surrendered and who was the patriarch of a family still active in the affairs of Lexington and Fayette County.

Leafland

SAMUEL T. HAYES HOUSE

ELEGANTLY SITUATED IN A GROVE OF TREES ON A COUNTRY ROAD AT THE WESTERN EDGE of Fayette County is a residence historically known as the Samuel T. Hayes House.

Facing north, the structure is a two-story, three-bay brick building with a hipped roof. A primitive but handsome datestone near the dentilated entablature on the rear ell has the initials of the builder and "1854," the year of construction. This basically Greek Revival-style house has a gracious and elaborate Tudor-style front portico, heralding a style of architecture that was soon to dot the Central Kentucky landscape. As described by architectural historian Clay Lancaster, the porch has "octagonal stone piers incorporated with traceried Tudor arches and railing around the upper deck, a central doorway upstairs as well as down." The double front door has etched glass; three paneled sidelights are angled and receded and, with the seven-pane transom, light the front hall.

The house was built by Samuel T. Hayes, a prosperous landowner. Obviously due to financial reversals, Mr. Hayes had to sell at public auction what the deed described as his "country residence." According to historian and writer Bettye Lee Mastin, the buyer was his nephew, Dr. George O. Graves, who, after having graduated as valedictorian at Centre College and with honors from the University of Pennsylvania Medical School, had seen his uncle's new house and "determined if his ability could do so he would some time own his farm."

The farm, which is presently known as Avondale, continues in the Bluegrass tradition with the breeding and raising of standardbred horses. The handsome Greek Revival house with its Gothic touches remains intact and represents the fine craftsmanship that flourished in Central Kentucky during that period.

Samuel T. Hayes House

ASHLAND

As early as 1804, Henry Clay, who was to become Kentucky's greatest
statesman, began acquisition of the land that he often referred to as his "beloved"
Ashland. Clay first gained national recognition as a leader of the "war hawks" in
Congress, later served as secretary of state, and was three times an unsuccessful
candidate for president of the United States. Ashland was his home from 1809
until his death in 1852.

There is evidence in deeds that there was a house on the land at the time it
was purchased by Clay. This could have been the structure to which Clay added
wings that were sketched by Benjamin Latrobe. In 1813 and 1814, there was a
correspondence to Clay from Latrobe concerning the design for the wings, but
there appears no mention of design for the main portion of the house. After
Clay's death, Ashland was purchased from the estate by his son, James B. Clay,
and in 1857, the original house was razed due to structural faults making it
unsafe. Reason would lead one to assume that the weaknesses in the house were
in the original main mass, which could have dated back to the 1790s and not in
the later Latrobe-designed wings.

The new Ashland was designed by Major Thomas Lewinski, and much of
the material from the original house was used in its reconstruction. It was built
on the same site, but the style of the building was changed. According to Clay
Lancaster, "Quoins were added at the corners, cornices made heavier, chimneys
elaborated, window headings arched, cast-iron hoods applied to those in the
principal block, sashes throughout filled with large panes of glass, a platform
placed in front of the entrance bay and a broad terrace at the back, and iron
balconies affixed to the front windows of the end pavilions."

Today, most of Clay's original 600-acre farm is a residential development.
The house and twenty acres are owned and maintained as an historic house
museum by the Henry Clay Memorial Foundation. Although not the exact house
that Henry Clay knew, several of the interesting original outbuildings are intact,
and the house is full of important Clay family memorabilia, much of which is
related to the lifetime of its great master.

As Elizabeth Simpson wrote, "Far across the reaches of the city the great
shaft of Clay's monument pierces the heavens, and on the summit the figure of
Lexington's own 'Henry of the West' faces east toward Ashland that he loved so
well."

Ashland

Parlor

MANSFIELD

MANSFIELD, LOCATED APPROXIMATELY TWO MILES EAST OF THE FAYETTE COUNTY Courthouse, was designed by Major Thomas Lewinski who, according to most architectural historians, made some of the greatest contributions to Kentucky architecture during the nineteenth century. The land was first owned by one of Lexington's founders, Levi Todd, and later by Colonel John Todd, who fell at the Battle of Blue Licks in 1782, popularly referred to as the last battle of the American Revolution.

One of the nation's best known political figures, Henry Clay, purchased the tract in 1837 and in 1845 had Mansfield built for his son, Thomas Hart Clay.

In its original form, Mansfield was a Greek Revival cottage with portico, pilasters, and full entablature, which, according to Clay Lancaster, "gave it a dignity in advance of its size." In 1927, under the ownership of Lexington entrepreneur John G. Stoll, wings were added, designed by one of Kentucky's best twentieth-century architects, Robert W. McMeekin.

Mansfield is one of the important residences in the Bluegrass region, not only because of its connection with the prominent Clay family but also for the artistic talents of two leading Kentucky architects.

CLOUD HOUSE

THIS TWO-STORY BRICK VILLA WAS BUILT FOR MRS. MARY CLOUD IN 1857 ON LAND which had been a 1,000-acre military survey awarded to Joseph Frazier in the late eighteenth century. Adjacent to it, on the east, is land once owned by the great Kentucky frontiersman, Simon Kenton. During several periods of ownership, it has been known as Cloverland, Trevilla, and now Bluegrass Farm.

This three-bay brick house has the imposing distinctiveness of the Greek Revival style and, according to Clay Lancaster, has "articulated chimney stacks and projecting bay windows which automatically put it into the romantic class." By the 1850s the Italianate style had begun creeping into the architectural scheme of the Bluegrass region, and the Cloud House is a fine example of the transition between this style and the earlier Greek Revival.

The only original outbuildings that remain are the ice house, in its original condition, and a carriage house, now remodeled, which serves as the office of one of the Bluegrass region's major horse farms. The owners, who live in Texas, continue the sensitive maintenance of this unique transitional house, which displays decorative elements from two nineteenth-century architectural styles.

CAVE SPRING

PROBABLY NO OTHER FARM COMPLEX IN KENTUCKY HAS AS MANY ORIGINAL BUILDINGS demonstrating the self-sufficiency of early farms as Cave Spring. Here one can find an early sequence of log, stone, and brick construction.

The main house was built by Captain Robert Boggs in the early 1790s. He first came to Kentucky in 1774 as a chain bearer for John Floyd, deputy surveyor of Virginia, and returned in 1775, when he helped erect the fort at Boonesborough. During this period, he claimed land that had a large spring issuing from a cave as the site for his future home, later named Cave Spring.

The Georgian-style house, constructed of stone, was built on gently sloping terrain resulting in three interior levels. The two rooms on the second story of the main block of the house are reached by separate stairways from the corresponding downstairs room. Originally separated from the main house was a large stone kitchen with a traveler's room above. The kitchen was connected to the main house by a covered, open-sided dogtrot that was enclosed about 1800 to make a dining room. In 1968, a stone wing was added to the north end of the house to accommodate a master-bedroom suite.

During the period 1784–1800, ancillary buildings also were constructed. Those remaining on the farm today, all in a fine state of repair, are the smokehouse, the hemp house, a brick cabin, a log house, and the icehouse. The Boggs family cemetery is located several hundred feet east of the main residence.

In the graveyard is a tall central monument containing the names of Robert and Sarah Huston Boggs and their children. Also inscribed is, "Settled on This Place, Feb. 18, 1784." Settled they did, for Cave Spring is owned by a direct descendant of Captain Robert Boggs and, except for one period, has been in the family for almost 200 years.

Cave Spring

Outbuilding

WINTON

THIS HOUSE IS A MONUMENT TO A GREAT KENTUCKY FAMILY THAT RESIDED HERE FOR more than 175 years. Major Samuel Meredith and his bride, Elizabeth Breckinridge, came to Kentucky from their family seat, Winton, in Amherst County, Virginia, to settle on land granted to his father, Samuel, Sr. The elder Meredith's wife was Jane Henry, sister of Patrick Henry who, as governor of Virginia, had the property surveyed.

Upon arriving in 1790, the family lived in a log house, which was followed by another log house and a brick structure. The main residence, essentially one-storied, was not constructed until 1823. Two of the early log structures, which were relocated when the main house was built, remain on the property. In 1866, the Merediths' daughter Letitia and her husband, Major William Dallam (a nephew of William Paca of Maryland, who was a signer of the Declaration of Independence), enlarged the house, principally with the addition of a second floor. During the period when Winton was occupied by Dallam's daughter and her husband, Dr. Robert Peter, many of the fields were converted to vineyards, and it is said that champagne was bottled on the place. Dr. Peter, besides being an outstanding surgeon, was a teacher and historian who must have preferred wine over the world-famous Kentucky whiskey.

In 1968, Winton was sold out of the family for the first time. Purchased by a prominent Lexington veterinarian and his family, Winton was renovated, added to, and its setting more manicured, in keeping with the image of Lexington's horse world. The wonderful old house still echoes with the memories of that early Kentucky family who crossed the Cumberland Gap to settle in the lush land of the Kentucky Bluegrass.

Outbuildings

Winton

CASTLE LAWN

Castle Lawn, located six miles southeast of Lexington, is an outstanding example of the Greek Revival style. It was built in 1847 for Benjamin McCann; the design and construction are credited to Lexington's first known architect-builder, John McMurtry. Little is known of McCann, although it is said that he came to Lexington from Tennessee to involve himself in the horse industry. He had assembled 300 acres from different purchases, including that part of the county originally known as the Locust Barren, a land grant to Levi Todd, grandfather to Mary Todd Lincoln. By 1860, Benjamin McCann had become financially overextended, sold the house and farm, and left the Bluegrass area.

This three-bay, two-story, classical brick house has all the boldness and high style of the Greek Revival period. The massive portico is supported by paired Ionic columns, and the main door is almost an exact copy of one in Minard Lafever's pattern book. According to Clay Lancaster, "The entablature with its frieze taken from the doorway on the north side of the Erechtheum on the Athenian Acropolis was duplicated twice in Fayette County doorways . . . at Waveland . . . and at the McCann house on the Richmond Pike."

Parlor

Castle Lawn

GRIMES HOUSE AND MILL

THE GRIMES FAMILY HOUSE AND MILL ARE LOCATED IN SOUTHEAST FAYETTE COUNTY on Boone Creek, which divides Fayette from Clark County. The buildings are a magnificent representation of the prosperous mill economy of early Kentucky that, in this instance, resulted in the building of these two architecturally significant structures. Clay Lancaster terms the Grimes House "the finest stone house existing in Fayette County."

Philip Grimes (1734–1809), born in Prince William County, Virginia, bought 225 acres of the Boone Creek land on May 1, 1798. He established his family in a log cabin and in 1803 hired an Irish stonemason, Peter Paul, who had recently established a business in Lexington, to construct a mill on the creek. In 1813, the date chiseled in a stone in the chimney, the magnificent residence was completed. It has been theorized by a present-day stonemason that the one-story ell was constructed in the 1790s, a two-story section added to this wing, and the main block of the house built last. The original front of the house, which is now considered the back, has alternating square and horizontal blocks reflecting the Flemish-bond pattern and is considered some of the finest stonework in Central Kentucky. The east gabled wing of this Georgian style house has four blind windows covered with closed shutters. Cornices have dentilated trim, and there is a water table surrounding the house. The interior trim is finely detailed, highlighted by niches on either side of the parlor fireplace.

The Grimes Mill is a massive two-and-one-half-story building constructed of quarried stone except for its framed gables. The east side of the mill has a large stone entrance under which the water from Boone Creek was originally channeled from the mill race to power the mill wheel. Not the original wooden wheel but a nineteenth-century iron mill wheel is still in place in the lower floor of the building.

The Grimes Mill is the clubhouse for the Iroquois Hunt. The hunt, formed in 1880, was named for the first American horse to win the English Derby. In 1928, Grimes Mill was selected as the site for their activities, and members ride to hounds twice a week during the season.

Grimes House

Blessing Of The Hounds At Grimes Mill

GRASSLAND

GRASSLAND IS ONE OF SIX HOUSES REMAINING IN FAYETTE COUNTY THAT WERE BUILT by sons and grandsons of Kentucky's first (and twice) governor, Isaac Shelby. Five of the six houses have been honored with National Register status, and all are on land that had been owned by the governor.

Located on a broad, flat area above the Shelby branch of East Hickman Creek, Grassland remains isolated from the surrounding farmland and commands the same view as it did in 1823. In keeping with the reputation for warm, genteel hospitality and the dapper bearing of Major Thomas Hart Shelby, son of Isaac Shelby and the builder of Grassland, the house has been referred to by Clay Lancaster as "the most gracious and best preserved domestic establishment in Fayette County." Susan Hart Shelby, Colonel Shelby's daughter-in-law and author of a book on life at Grassland, said that no one ever spoke of Colonel Shelby "without mentioning his white pants and wine-colored vests." She went on to describe life at Grassland "as the basis for any Bluegrass Antebellum novel: warm friendly life, wealth and graciousness, children initiated early into the romance of the hunt and the dance."

Grassland was designed by Lexington's first self-proclaimed architect, Matthew Kennedy. The proportions are refined, and its façade is laid in Flemish bond, with a foundation of smooth-faced cut stone and a superimposed colossal order. The central entrance bay is accented by a triple window on the second floor and a simple but elegant doorpiece below, highlighted by an elliptical leaded-glass fanlight. Four of Grassland's original outbuildings remain.

In all aspects—proportions, ornament, plan, and placement of dependencies—Grassland mirrors the personal qualities of its builder; moreover, his decision to engage the services of an architect at this early date, in addition to his being primarily a farmer living isolated in the country, is again indicative of his gracious and sophisticated mien.

Grassland

WOODSTOCK

WILLIAM HAYES, WHO HAD MIGRATED TO KENTUCKY FROM MARYLAND, BUILT A story-and-one-half brick house on the Todds Road in Fayette County. Inscribed on a brick in the southwest chimney are the owner's initial and date of construction, "H 1812." The days of those first settlers were, according to Robert Peter's 1882 history of Fayette County, "The days of early pioneer effort, when the settler was of necessity a soldier, the farmer a fighter of Indians: when hearth and homes and crops and flocks were in constant hazard, and were only held as the hard-won reward of eternal vigilance, alike of women and men."

Woodstock's central unit features brick laid in Flemish bond and windows with twelve-over-twelve sashes. This main block was constructed first but was closely followed by one-story wings on either side. The chimney at the end of the later west wing has a brick marked "H 1820." This Federal-style house has an interior stairway similar to many found in small houses in Maryland but unique for the Bluegrass region.

Over the years, the wings have been modified to accommodate more modern living. Nevertheless, Woodstock, situated on a small rise fronted with old locust trees and white fences, stands as a fine example of the building expertise of many early settlers of Kentucky.

LEXINGTON'S GRATZ PARK

Gratz Park presents one of the most serene and charming historic settings in all America. Clay Lancaster, nationally-known architectural historian, has called Gratz Park "The Louisburg Square of Lexington." Lancaster continues, "There is still no more pleasant place to be found in Lexington than Gratz Park. With the Hunt and Bodley houses facing each other at Second [Street] and the alignment of beautifully scaled residences up Mill and Market [Streets], one finds here the manifestation of satisfying balance without staid formality. The park has charm, atmosphere, a sense of tranquility and of history, and it provides an oasis of planting tucked into the city scape. Gratz Park is a treasured gem; it would require a century and one-half of intelligent planning and natural growth to be equaled. May it be preserved for the edification and delight of future generations."

Gratz Park had its beginnings in 1781 as Out Lot No. 6 when the town plat of Lexington was prepared at the order of the Virginia Assembly. In 1793 a group of Lexingtonians purchased Out Lot No. 6 for a seminary (later to become Transylvania University) and erected on it a two-story building. In 1818 a handsome three-story structure, designed by Lexington's first architect, Matthew Kennedy, was built. This Federal-style building burned in 1829, when Cassius Clay's servant, who had been blacking his master's boots, fell asleep, unaware that a candle had been left burning. In 1833, the university moved across Third Street to higher ground where Gideon Shryock had erected the majestic Greek Revival Morrison College.

H. H. Gratz leased the old campus from the university in 1875 as a centennial park for the City of Lexington. His father, Benjamin Gratz, had come to Lexington and in 1824 acquired a house facing the college green. Benjamin Gratz was a member of a prominent Philadelphia family, and his beautiful sister, Rebecca, reputedly was the inspiration for Rebecca of Sir Walter Scott's *Ivanhoe*. Today Gratz Park is a city park with one of the original Transylvania buildings remaining. This small one-story brick structure is known as the "Kitchen," denoting its probable original use when the park served as the university campus. In 1904–6 the city library, built with funds donated by Andrew Carnegie, was constructed on the south quarter of Gratz Park. Unfortunately, although it added

James Lane Allen Foundation

to the cultural aspect of the city, the building visually closed that end of the park.

Gratz Park and its buildings have borne the seasons well. Long before historic preservation had become popular, the houses facing the park were prestigious addresses for many of the better families who settled the area. As any other inner-city residential area, though, it has seen both good and bad times. The latter occurred in 1954 when the John Bradford house, located on the southwest corner of Mill and Second, was razed to make way for parking. Bradford had brought the first printing press west of the Alleghenies and had resided in this house for a number of years. Earlier, it had been the home of Colonel Thomas Hart and the site of the wedding of Hart's daughter, Lucretia, to Henry Clay.

Because of this great loss, a small group of shocked citizens organized The Blue Grass Trust for Historic Preservation and purchased Hopemont, the beautiful Federal house of the Hunts and Morgans, across the street from the Bradford house. It, too, was endangered. Hopemont, now more commonly known as the Hunt-Morgan House, was built in 1814 by one of Lexington's most prominent citizens, John Wesley Hunt, and was the last home of his grandson, the famous Confederate general John Hunt Morgan—"The Thunderbolt of the Confederacy"—who was killed during the Civil War. Thomas Hunt Morgan, renowned geneticist and Kentucky's first Nobel Prize winner (1933), was born at Hopemont, which today is operated as a house museum.

Much has been lost, but there are still many fine buildings that must be saved if the character of Lexington and the surrounding area is to be retained. Two organizations in Fayette County, The Blue Grass Trust for Historic

Dudley House

Morrison Hall
Transylvania University

Preservation and The Lexington-Fayette County Historic Commission, continue their efforts to save the best of the past for future generations, keeping in mind that "progress" continues and preserved buildings must have adaptive uses that suit the present-day scheme of life in the city. With Gratz Park as its anchor, Lexington and Fayette County continue to lead the way in retaining the visual beauty of the Bluegrass region.

Gratz House

Market Street

Bodley House

Market Street

HUNT-MORGAN HOUSE

THERE ARE FEW BUILDINGS IN THE BLUEGRASS REGION THAT ARE CHERISHED MORE than the Hunt-Morgan House. After its construction in 1814, the house was the scene of much of the business, political, and social life of Lexington. Its builder, John Wesley Hunt, who came to Kentucky from Trenton, New Jersey, and achieved success in the business world of the new west, is reputed to have become the first millionaire in the commonwealth.

Hunt and his wife, Catherine Grosh (niece of Francis Scott Key, the author of our national anthem), had twelve children. Their daughter Henrietta married Calvin Morgan, and it was their son, John Hunt Morgan, who rose to the rank of brigadier general during the Civil War and whose guerrilla style of warfare made him famous as the "Thunderbolt of the Confederacy." The daring raids of Morgan and his men did much to keep up the spirits of Southerners during some of the darker days of this bloody conflict.

Lexingtonians were divided in their allegiance to the Confederacy and the Union. Although Kentucky sought to be a neutral state during the war, residents of the Bluegrass region had more sympathy for the Southern cause, and Lexington was truly a city of "brother against brother." It is said that whenever General Morgan would ride into town to see his family, neighbor Benjamin Gratz would rush to the courthouse and insist that an indictment of treason be issued against the general. Another story is that General Morgan rode into Lexington being pursued by Union soldiers. Arriving at the front of the family house on his famous mare, Black Bess, he rode up the front steps, through the house where he kissed his mother, and out the back door.

The most memorable architectural feature of the Hunt-Morgan House is its impressive doorway of exceptional size. Both the sidelights and the fan above have leaded glass that flows into a charming pattern, giving the facade an exuberant design element. Considered a Kentucky adaptation of the Federal style, the house shows the creativity of early Bluegrass builders. The woodwork features reeded window and door jambs with corner blocks having a circular design. The woodwork in the house might have been done by the famous early Mercer County craftsman, Matthew Lowry, who was noted for the quality of his workmanship, especially his bold and beautifully carved mantels. The drawing room has windows which come to floor level and probably had triple sashes, allowing guests to step through into the garden. Along the Second Street side of the house, Mr. Hunt had a six-foot-high brick wall built, creating a courtyard to protect his family from the busy street. The courtyard, a feature adapted from the styles of the deeper South, is unusual in the Bluegrass.

The imposing Hunt-Morgan House is the headquarters for The Blue Grass Trust for Historic Preservation. Parts of it have been restored, and guided tours are conducted on a regular basis. The house is also used on a limited scale for social functions.On an evening when the house is being used for entertainment, the lovely glass hall lantern shines through the fanlight, and the passerby begins to understand how the great doorways of Bluegrass mansions symbolize the Kentucky tradition of hospitality.

Hunt-Morgan House

The Dining Room with Portraits
of Mr. and Mrs. Hunt

CASTLETON

CASTLETON FARM WAS ONCE PART OF THE VAST ESTATE OF JOHN BRECKINRIDGE, WHO came to Kentucky with his wife, Mary Cabell, and children from Albemarle County, Virginia, in 1793. He soon owned nearly 2,500 acres, which he called Cabell's Dale in honor of his wife. Breckinridge became a United States senator and at the time of his premature death in 1806, was attorney general in the cabinet of Thomas Jefferson. He died at Cabell's Dale, leaving his young wife prostrate with grief. Until her death a half-century later, she wore a black cap, which earned her the nickname of "Grandma Black Cap." She became blind soon after her husband's death, and it has been a family tradition that she had cried her eyes out.

David Castleman, who had married John and Mary Breckinridge's daughter, Mary Ann, inherited his wife's 446-acre share of the estate upon her death. In 1841, he planned and built the fine Greek Revival house called Castleton. An early drawing shows Castleton with a massive portico rather than the smaller front porch which now adorns the house. The present porch, as described by Clay Lancaster, has columns of the Ionic order. Those sustaining the portico itself are cut from stone, probably a late nineteenth-century replacement, contemporary with the terraces on either side. Castleton is a large square mass with a hipped roof and a recessed Greek Revival front doorway; a similar recessed doorway exits to the porch roof from the second story.

Castleton has always been associated with the horse industry. Dr. Mary Wharton, contributing author of *The Horse World of the Bluegrass*, says, "For over a century and a half Castleton has had a glorious history in the horse world, from the thoroughbreds of the Breckinridges through the saddlers of the Castlemans, the trotters of the Fords, the thoroughbreds of James R. Keene, the standardbreds of David Look and finally to the saddlebreds and standardbreds of Frances Dodge Van Lennep and Frederick L. Van Lennep. . . . Thus, Castleton Farm, bigger than ever before, remains true to its 190-year-old tradition of quality."

Castleton

The Old Slave Cabin

POPLAR GROVE

LOCATED ON A HORSE FARM ONLY FOUR MILES FROM DOWNTOWN LEXINGTON, AND situated on a slight rise in a grove of trees, Poplar Grove belongs to a small group of early Central Kentucky houses whose builders were beginning to have an awareness of interior spatial design. The result is an effective use of space that creates a sense of proportions larger than one would expect to find in this small house.

Details of design in both the exterior and interior are rather casual. The windows are not equal in distance from the pedimented entrance pavilion with its wide fan door. The gracious arch between the front and back halls is not centered, nor is the parlor fireplace, a casualness resulting from the effort to create a more open interior design. According to architectural historian Clay Lancaster, "This consciousness of spatial design foreshadowed the Greek Revival but it shows here as an indigenous development, unaccompanied by the stylistic innovations which characterized the later movement."

This small Federal-style brick house was built ca. 1810 by William Sullivan, who purchased several hundred acres along South Elkhorn Creek. The land and house stayed in his family until the first quarter of this century. A granddaughter of William Sullivan married Joseph Frazier, and for many years it was known locally as the "old Frazier place."

After standing vacant for many years, this charming house was recently rescued by the son of its last owner, who had purchased the farm in 1917. Poplar Grove has been carefully rehabilitated and returned to its rightful position as one of the important smaller houses in the Bluegrass.

Poplar Grove

Center Hall

OAKLAND

HORACE COLEMAN WAS NOT YET OF AGE WHEN HIS FATHER ALLOWED HIM TO COME TO Kentucky from Spottsylvania County, Virginia, in a covered wagon with his aunt, Franky (Frances Coleman) Graves. She was the widow of Joseph Graves and took the long journey over the mountains into Kentucky with nine of her ten children and her nephew Horace. The story is told that young Horace brought with him several slaves who had been trained to make and lay brick and after his arrival engaged himself in the house-building trade. It was he who built Oakland, and attributed to his skill are several other houses in the area.

Oakland, as are the other houses said to be built by Coleman, is one-and-one-half stories with its façade "laid up" in the Flemish-bond brick pattern. Occasionally the footprint of a deer or fox can be seen in one of the bricks, for in days gone by animals would sometimes cross a field where bricks were drying in the open field. One of the unusual features of his houses is that there are no stone foundations, for he used brick for that purpose. Oakland has double front doors leading into twin parlors which house much of the woodwork installed when the house was built ca. 1820.

Soon the Graveses and the Colemans and their descendants owned thousands of acres in the area now known as Pine Grove. The land, some of the richest in Kentucky, is gently rolling, with spring-fed streams that are tributaries of Boone Creek. Much of it still belongs to relatives of the original settlers. One of these families has bedroom furniture made from the cherry logs that were used to construct the log house of the original Franky Graves.

Oakland, which is more than a mile off the road, housed tenants for over fifty years and was vacant for seventeen years before the house and twelve acres were purchased in 1972 by E.I. Thompson, a Lexington realtor, auctioneer, raconteur, and historian. Painstakingly, he and his wife renovated the house, thus saving another part of Bluegrass architectural heritage. During the renovation period, a creek in the field next to the house was dammed, creating a one-acre lake which offers a resting place for migratory water fowl. The present owner, a gracious lady who now calls the place Pebblebrook, continues the maintenance of this Kentucky landmark that was nearly lost due to neglect.

Oakland

Front Portico

BOTHERUM

BOTHERUM IS ONE OF THE GEMS OF AMERICA DOMESTIC ARCHITECTURE. IN 1851, Madison Conyers Johnson commissioned Lexington's well-known architect-builder John McMurtry to design and erect this small-scale Greek temple with its Gothic mode interior. The combination of these Classical revival styles resulted in one of the more unusual houses in the Bluegrass. From its beginning, the house was known as Botherum, and it is said that it was named for Counsel Botherum, a character in a play by Thomas Fielding.

The house was originally situated on thirty acres at the edge of Lexington and faced High Street. Times changed, and the environs of Botherum changed as well. Urban encroachment cut away its long approach to High Street and Botherum is now reached from a side street appropriately called Madison Place. The setting changed, but the house, well cared for today by its present owner, is still a fitting abode for any Kentucky gentleman.

Except for a few details, the exterior is Greek Revival, with Corinthian columns supporting pedimented porticoes and with pilasters along the walls. Upon entering, one views an interior that is wholly Gothic Revival. The octagonal drawing room has a high-vaulted ceiling featuring a rectangular centerpiece elaborately decorated with flowers and vines molded in plaster. The windows have diamond-shaped panes, as do interior doors in which some of the glass is colored. Whether this compatible mixture of styles should be credited to the builder McMurtry or to the owner Madison Johnson is not known, but the result is a charming, romantic cottage that has few equals.

Major Johnson was brilliant and eccentric. In 1823, at the age of fifteen, he graduated from Transylvania University with highest honors. He was valedictorian of his class, but he did not attend the ceremony to receive his diploma. His speech was read by someone else, for it is said that he thought himself too physically ugly to participate in the ceremony. In spite of this lifelong complex, he became a brilliant lawyer, was a confidant of Henry Clay, and married Sally Anne Clay, a sister of General Cassius Marcellus Clay. His wife died after a year of marriage, and he remained true to the love of his youth until his death. Lexington author James Lane Allen wrote a delightful short story called "Two Gentlemen of Kentucky," and Major Johnson and his manservant were the prototypes for Colonel Romulus Fields and his faithful servant Peter Cotton, the main characters of the story.

The turn-of-the-century neighborhood that developed on Johnson's estate is known now as Woodward Heights and recently was placed on the National Register of Historic Places. Botherum has lost its original dramatic setting, but it is still shaded by the large gingko tree, which, tradition has it, was a gift to Madison Johnson from his friend Henry Clay. Botherum stands as a reminder of the structures and the people who were part of the city that once was known as the Athens of the West.

Botherum

STONY POINT

STONY POINT WAS BUILT IN THE 1790S BY CAPTAIN JOHN PARKER ON THE PARKER'S Mill Road in Fayette County. The major features are mostly intact after almost 200 years, but the present owners struggle for survival of the house because of its proximity to Bluegrass Field, Lexington's airport.

John Parker was born in 1753 near Valley Forge, Pennsylvania, and went to Virginia in 1774, where he lived until he joined the Minutemen under Colonel Samuel Meredith. He was commissioned a captain in the Revolutionary Army and most likely fought in 1779 at the Battle of Stony Point, New York, for which he later named his house. After the war, Captain Parker came to Kentucky and settled on the banks of South Elkhorn Creek, where he operated a grist mill. He soon became a prominent citizen and served as a town trustee, a county magistrate, and a Kentucky legislator.

Situated part way up a slope, the two-story brick house has a later Greek Revival portico but has the early architectural features of a belt course and a water table not found in the Bluegrass after the first quarter of the nineteenth century. As was customary at the time the front wall is laid in Flemish-bond brickwork while the others are in common bond. Still intact are pegged window frames, even those on a two-story wing, which indicates its early construction date.

A dry stack fence separates the road from the yard, which has an abundance of handsome large trees and shrubs. The serenity of this setting is periodically interrupted by jet planes landing at the airport, but Stony Point stands as a reminder of the solid and pleasing structures of many of the early Kentucky settlers.

WALNUT HILL CHURCH

SEVEN YEARS BEFORE KENTUCKY BECAME A STATE, THE WALNUT HILL PRESBYTERIAN Church was established in a then-remote corner of Fayette County. The year was 1785 and the building was a log structure on land given by General Levi Todd, Kentucky frontiersman, who had fought at the Siege of Bryan Station and the Battle of Blue Licks and who was the grandfather of Mary Todd Lincoln.

In 1801, the present forty-by-fifty-foot structure was erected, and it has the distinction of being the oldest Presbyterian church building in Kentucky. This historic stone church is nearly the same as originally built, except for an 1880s remodeling, which introduced windows in the Gothic style and removed the interior slave galleries.

Services were held until 1953. In 1972, a committee was formed, principally from that part of the county, to renovate the building and to resume worship. In December 1975, the church was rededicated, and today it has an active congregation planning the construction of a stone parish house.

Situated on a thirteen-acre knoll of beautiful Bluegrass land dotted with stately trees, the Walnut Hill Church is vibrant again with hymns and prayers. Its original simple Georgian style blends harmoniously with its later Gothic alterations, making it one of the most historic and charming buildings in the commonwealth.

MORTON HOUSE

Erected in 1810 by William "Lord" Morton, this house follows the sprawling, one-story concept often used by Thomas Jefferson.

William Morton had come to Lexington in 1788 from Baltimore and established a number of businesses that soon provided him with the wealth to build this impressive house. The title, "Lord" Morton, as he was often called by his fellow citizens, was not inherited but derived from his grand manner and scale of living.

The Federal-style house is a five-part pavilion composition with hipped roofs on the three major sections. The flat deck on the roof of the main block is enclosed with a railing. Unusual in Kentucky are the stuccoed brick walls, scored to resemble stone, with simulated quoins at the corners. Two small pavilions, which originally had false doors, connect the main block of the house with the outer wings.

The house sits well back from Limestone Street at the corner of Fifth Street. The entrance door, nearly ten feet high, and the two Palladian-style windows on either side, almost eight feet wide, give the passerby the impression of a larger-scale building. A dogwood blossom motif embossed on the frieze was originally found on the window and door frames as well. In the two front rooms, the same design is carried out on the marble mantels, unusual features for this early period.

Cassius Marcellus Clay purchased the Morton property in 1836 for $18,000, and it was here that he and his family lived until 1850, when they moved to the Clay family estate in Madison County known as White Hall. Clay was a fiery abolitionist, and it was during the period in which he resided at Morton House that he published his controversial antislavery newspaper, *The True American*. Clay was appointed U.S. ambassador to Russia by President Lincoln and for a short time served the Union as a major general. In his autobiography, Clay described Morton House as "the most elegant in the city."

Later the property passed into other ownership. In 1913, it was given to the city and is known as Duncan Park after the family who donated it. Recently the house was partly renovated by the Lexington-Fayette Urban County Government, and plans are underway to use it for a black history museum and cultural center.

Morton House

THOMAS B. WATKINS HOUSE

THE THOMAS B. WATKINS HOUSE, ON SOUTH BROADWAY, IS ONE OF THE BEST documented of the later works of Lexington's prolific architect-builder, John McMurtry. He designed and built it in 1887 for his daughter and son-in-law, Thomas B. Watkins, a prosperous shoe merchant and a nephew of statesman Henry Clay. Members of the McMurtry family lived here until 1978.

In 1833, John McMurtry, then twenty years old, came to Kentucky from Maryland with his family. For more than half a century, he was the most active builder in the area and, after the Civil War, was probably the leading architect in the Bluegrass region. McMurtry was responsible for many of the great Greek Revival houses so numerous in this area, and he went on to disseminate the Gothic Revival throughout the Bluegrass after having built in the Greek, Roman, and Italianate manners. There is no question that he was one of the major shapers of Lexington's nineteenth-century environment.

The Watkins House includes elements of Italianate, Gothic Revival, and Eastlake styles. According to architectural historian Walter Langsam, "The Watkins House is in many ways typical of its period, yet has several subtle distinctive features, probably derived from the architect's intimate knowledge of the needs and preferences of the clients." Among these needs was the "family" room and the master bedroom above it, and the adjacent nursery and bathroom downstairs, at the expense of formal parlors.

The years saw the transition of this once-residential neighborhood into a commercial area, the Watkins house finally being surrounded by tobacco warehouses. This Lexington landmark was left vacant after 1978, and little hope was given for its survival. However, in 1981 the property was purchased by an astute businessman who saw the possibilities of renovating the house as an office building, especially in view of advantageous tax credits. It was adapted to its new use with very few changes in the basic integrity of the house, and again it draws the admiration of Lexingtonians.

Thomas B. Watkins House

FLORAL HALL

IN SEVERAL CITIES THROUGHOUT OUR COUNTRY, ONE CAN FIND OCTAGONAL BUILDINGS to which local citizens point with pride. In Lexington, Floral Hall is such a building and is a symbol of The Red Mile Trotting Track. This imposing structure was built in 1882 near the track that has seen some of the world's greatest standardbred horse racing since the 1870s. Today The Red Mile is regarded as the fastest of all tracks for the sport of harness racing.

In 1861, the Kentucky Agricultural and Mechanical Association purchased this land off South Broadway, laid out a race course, and built an elaborate grandstand. In 1872, it held its first annual fair on the site, and ten years later Lexington architect-builder John McMurtry built Floral Hall for horticultural and agricultural exhibitions. It originally had two floors of display space, and it proved to be a popular meeting spot during the Agricultural and Mechanical Association fairs.

By the 1890s, Floral Hall had been converted to a horse barn. For many years it was called the round barn or the Berry barn after Tom Berry, the noted English trainer who stabled his horses there. The building deteriorated over the years, but in 1971 extensive renovations were completed and the owners chartered it as a museum to be known as The Stable of Memories. It is occasionally used by various civic organizations for fund-raising activities.

Whatever its use, it will always be Floral Hall to many Lexingtonians, the picturesque octagonal building out at the trotting track.

Floral Hall

LEMON HILL

LEMON HILL IS AN INTRIGUING EXAMPLE OF GREEK REVIVAL FORMALITY MIXED WITH the informality and practical design of an earlier country house. During the 1840s, when the house was built, many of the great Greek Revival mansions were appearing in the Bluegrass, and their owners, architects, and builders usually carried the formal design throughout. Lemon Hill was an exception, and the variances give it a unique charm.

Abraham Lunsford Ferguson, the builder of Lemon Hill, must not have concerned himself much with fashion. The front of the house, built on a smooth-faced ashlar foundation, has all the elements of a full-block Greek Revival mansion. According to architectural historian Clay Lancaster, "Despite its superficial dressiness, Lemon Hill is a genuine country house. In some respects it is more satisfying from the rear view, where the formal elements are not in evidence. Here, one would hardly suspect the house of belonging to the Greek Revival era, and might place it two decades later."

At the front, one enters a deep room, which has the width of the main block of the house. This impressive space appears symmetrical, with the location of a blind door on the rear wall to match another that leads to the stairhall. The interior side of the entrance doorway has the same elaborate treatment as the exterior. A large floral plaster ceiling piece crowns the rest of the ornate detailing of this room.

There are two other design treatments not found elsewhere in the Bluegrass region. One is an original cast-iron railing, which has a stylized geometric design, between the columns of the massive front portico. In addition, the two wings have two stories but show second-story windows only on the sides, thus appearing as one-storied from the front.

Abraham Ferguson, whose family claimed descent from Scotland's first crowned head, King Fergus, came from Fauquier County, Virginia, in 1785, bringing his seventeen-year-old bride Nancy into the wilderness of Kentucky, and together they claimed lands granted him for military service. The family soon outgrew the log house, and Abraham expanded it into a larger stone house. After Abraham's death in 1840, his son, who had five sons and a daughter, built Lemon Hill. The house was sold out of the Ferguson family in 1905. In 1978, Lemon Hill was sold again after having been used as a tenant house for almost forty years, and the new owners are slowly bringing it back to its former glory with the same effort shown by those early, dauntless pioneers.

Lemon Hill

Parlor

61

WALNUT HALL

WALNUT HALL WAS BUILT ON LAND THAT WAS A GRANT OF ONE THOUSAND ACRES issued in 1777 to Colonel William Christian for his military service during the Revolutionary War. Christian County in southern Kentucky was named for the colonel, who was granted a total of nine thousand acres in Kentucky. He married Ann Henry, younger sister of Patrick, at her father's estate, Mt. Brilliant, in Virginia. In 1816, four hundred of the one thousand acres in the Bluegrass was sold to Matthew Flournoy, a member of a French Huguenot family whose name was an anglicization of *Fleur Noir*.

Built of brick, the present house was begun in 1842 by Matthew Flournoy's son Victor. The woodwork was milled from the abundance of walnut trees on the land. The façade of the main body of the house consists of five bays raised on a high podium. These openings are evenly spaced between five brick pilasters. The square mass is fronted by a two-story, tetra-style Doric portico. The hipped roof originally had only a railing at its summit, and in the 1890s, the present belvedere was added, as were the two-story wings on both sides of the original house. Wrought-iron railings were added to the portico and steps, and cast-iron figures of females holding lanterns were placed at the base of the front steps. The lantern bearers are a decorative feature now often connected with the house.

There were two other owners of Walnut Hall after it was sold out of the Flournoy family in 1879 and before it was purchased by Lamon V. Harkness in 1892. It was Harkness' father Stephen who had financially backed John D. Rockefeller when he started the Standard Oil Company. The Harkness family established Walnut Hall as one of the world's finest standardbred breeding farms, and it remains in that class today and still under the same family ownership.

Walnut Hall

Lamps at Front Steps

CLEVELAND-ROGERS HOUSE

THIS FINE FEDERAL-STYLE HOUSE HAS LONG BEEN REFERRED TO BY THE NAMES OF THE two families who were the first owners of the land. It was this tract in southeast Fayette County, bordered on three sides by the Kentucky River and the fourth side by Boone Creek, that Eli Cleveland bought and where he built two log cabins in the late eighteenth century. Cleveland was a magistrate in Fayette County in 1792 and also owned the first mill in the area, which burned in 1796.

In 1819, Cleveland sold the property to Joseph Hale Rogers and his son Jeremiah. Joseph Rogers had come to Kentucky from Culpeper County, Virginia, in 1784 and settled at Bryan Station, where he already owned more than 4,000 acres. Immediately upon the purchase of the Cleveland place, his son Jeremiah started the construction of the house that stands today; it was completed in 1820. The house and farm remained in the Rogers family until bought by the present owner's family in 1910. The Cleveland-Rogers House is a one-and-one-half-story, five-bay brick dwelling with the principal façade laid in Flemish bond. The massing, floor plan, exterior and interior trim, front porch, and openings are all characteristic of the Federal period. The windows and door on the front have reeded moldings with corner blocks. The rear door is treated in a similar manner. The interior is richly embellished with some of the finest carved woodwork in the region.

The Rogers house, the Cleveland cabins, the brick smokehouse, and an early log barn make up a complex of early Kentucky buildings on land that has been owned by only three families. The main house with its refined details is undisputed as an antebellum treasure in the Bluegrass.

Cleveland-Rogers House

HELM PLACE

Dramatically situated on a hill just off the Harrodsburg Pike, Helm Place is an exceptional house both architecturally and historically. Once the site of Todd's Station, a fort established by Levi Todd in 1779, the land passed into the hands of Colonel Abraham Bowman through a military grant, and he soon acquired 8,000 additional acres. His farm was known as Cedar Hill after the Bowman estate in Virginia. Colonel Bowman commanded the Eighth Virginia Infantry during the Revolutionary War and served directly under the Marquis de Lafayette. Both Colonel Bowman and the marquis were wounded at the Battle of Brandywine Creek, and when Lafayette visited Lexington in 1825 during his triumphant visit to America, the two men rode together in a carriage during the welcoming ceremonies.

It has been said that Helm Place was built by Colonel Bowman, but it appears more reasonable to believe that it was built by his son, George Bowman, after he, along with his mother, inherited the major part of the colonel's estate in 1837. It is probably safe to assume that the house was built in the 1840s, which would correspond to the blossoming of the Greek Revival style in the Bluegrass.

According to architectural historian Patrick Snadon,

> The order of the house is simplified and monumental Ionic, the four columns of the colossal portico being brick with plaster. The columns are intentionally spaced so as to leave the widest span in the center, and by this means, to stress both the central axis of the facade and to throw notice upon the elaborate frontispiece consisting of Ionic pilasters, entablature, side light and transom. . . . It is a particularly important example of the domestic Greek Revival in Central Kentucky; at once illustrating both forms and techniques indigenous to the region in which it was built, and influences from outside sources acting on the region, as examplified by the Eastern Architectural Pattern Books, which formed the single most important outside influence upon the Greek Revival style in Central Kentucky.

In 1912, Emilie Todd Helm, widow of Confederate General Benjamin Hardin Helm and half-sister to Mary Todd Lincoln, bought the property. Since that time, it has been known as Helm Place.

After her husband was killed in the Battle of Chickamauga, Emilie was invited to live with her half-sister and her husband Abraham Lincoln in the White House. Criticized for this kind gesture towards his sister-in-law, the president said: "My wife and I are in the habit of choosing our own guests. . . . The little 'rebel' came because I ordered her to come."

The Helm family sold Helm Place in 1946 to the prominent Lexington attorney and nationally-known Lincoln scholar, William H. Townsend. Today, this stately house is occupied by his family, which keeps alive the traditions of the Bowmans and the Helms.

Helm Place

Front Hall

JAMES LANE ALLEN HOUSE

No one loved Kentucky more than James Lane Allen, and no one made Kentucky more beloved than he did through his books. James Lane Allen was Kentucky's best-known author during the last quarter of the nineteenth and first quarter of the twentieth centuries. His stories recalled the place of his birth, for many of them tell about the early history of Lexington and life in Kentucky during those times. He wrote about court days, auctions, horse trading, hemp farming, stock sales, and bird lore.

Allen wrote more than one hundred and twenty-five novels, short stories, essays, criticisms, and travelogues. His fame in the United States was as widespread as his stories, which were published in the most popular magazines of that day. He wrote, "Behind all that I have written lie the landscapes of a single neighborhood." This neighborhood was the farm and house, now known as Scarlet Gate, in which he lived during the formative years of his life.

The James Lane Allen house, built ca. 1795, was originally in the two-story Federal style. The main block of the present structure was one room deep with two rooms on each floor. It has Flemish bond brickwork on the facade, common bond on the later additions, and a stone foundation. Under the gabled roof of the main section, the rafters are numbered and joined with wooden pegs. The author described his home place as a "brick house of the Virginia pattern . . . a very good one for that time."

Over the years the house has been greatly enlarged, but the remodeling was done in scale and with materials that made it very pleasing and comfortable. Although the area of Lexington in which it is located has been subdivided and heavily populated for many years, Scarlet Gate, surrounded by stately old trees in a twenty-acre, park-like setting, harkens back to an earlier Kentucky.

James Lane Allen House

MOUNT BRILLIANT

OF ALL THE HOUSES IN THE BLUEGRASS REGION, IT COULD BE SAID THAT MOUNT Brilliant holds a place closest to the hearts of many Lexingtonians. The house was started during the last decade of the eighteenth century for William Russell, on land that originally had been granted to his uncle by Thomas Jefferson in 1774.

William Russell and his brother Robert journeyed west from their native Culpeper County, Virginia, to claim the land. William built his house, naming it Mount Brilliant after the estate of his family's friend, Patrick Henry. Robert claimed the adjoining land to the north and called his place Poplar Hill. Although William Russell's tract had fewer acres than his brother's, he had on his property the never-failing spring that runs out of an uncharted cavern known as Russell Cave. The road that runs in front of the house and the spring is called the Russell Cave Pike.

There are two early structures at Mount Brilliant. It is said that the earlier was started in 1786 and is now the nucleus of the present guest house. A 1796 two-story brick structure is incorporated in the main house. It was originally five-bayed with a central hall and one room on either side. The present house has nine bays on the front and accommodates four rooms across. During the Greek Revival period, the massive Doric-columned portico was added.

From its earliest days, Mount Brilliant was a place of activity and note-worthiness in the annals of Bluegrass history. As early as 1807, Fortescue Cuming wrote in his *Sketches of a Tour to the Western Country* that Mount Brilliant was surrounded by a wall with turrets at each end next to the road and that "the tout ensemble [wanted] only the vineyards to resemble the country habitations of Languedoc and Provence."

Meetings and barbecues were often held at Mount Brilliant. It was at a political rally here in the summer of 1843 that Cassius M. Clay, noted anti-slavery leader, had his famous encounter with Samuel Brown from New Orleans. The story is told that while Clay was heckling a speaker, he was knocked down from behind by Brown. While drawing his famous bowie knife, Clay was shot from arm's length. Clay would have been shot in the heart except that the bullet was deflected by the scabbard of his knife, leaving only a red spot on his chest. Enraged, Clay cut off Brown's ear, gouged out one of his eyes, split his head open, and threw him over the fence into the water of Russell Cave. Both men lived. Cassius Clay was tried for mayhem and defended in court by his cousin Henry Clay, who based his legal argument on the premise that Cassius was only acting in the manner befitting a Kentuckian. The jury agreed with the persuasive attorney.

Since 1915, this great Bluegrass estate has been owned by the well-known Haggin family of Central Kentucky. They sponsor a number of lively political and charitable events each year so that many people still have an opportunity to experience the graciousness which has been synonymous with Mount Brilliant since the eighteenth century.

Mount Brilliant

TODHUNTER HOUSE

ON A FARM THAT STRADDLES THE FAYETTE AND JESSAMINE LINES STANDS A FINE Greek Revival-style residence built in the 1840s for John S. Todhunter. The 1904 publication *Country Estates of the Blue Grass* says, "The house which stands upon a grassy prominence, is a type of the commodious square solid structure that has made Central Kentucky famous for substantial homesteads. Shrubs and trees of every description surround the house and beautify the sloping lawn. Woodland trees shade the meadows, and a picturesque drive leads to the door steps. . . . The neighborhood is one of hereditary country gentlemen." Much of that description holds true today.

The Greek Revival style of the house is fairly typical. It is described in the *Survey of Historic Sites in Kentucky — Jessamine County* as follows: "The facade is distinguished by the triple windows, central doors on both floors and a denticulated cornice. Both doors have fluted Doric columns but the upper door is deemphasized by a crossetted architrave while that on first level consists of a full pilaster entablature arrangement." The vertical arrangement of the second-story door above the main entrance is seen in several houses of this period in the region.

The Todhunter family sold the property in 1858. In 1876 it was purchased by Ambrose Young, who owned large tracts of land in that section of the Bluegrass, and it remained in the same family for almost one hundred years. The present owners, who have a well-known stable of saddlebred horses, remodeled the old place, which had been known for many years as Locust Heights. The renovation included converting a two-room log building at the side of the main house into guest quarters. Tradition has it that this log building was once a tavern run by Abraham Venable, a veteran of the Revolutionary War.

This once-peaceful country pike today has become more populated. There are few if any "hereditary country gentlemen" left, but the Todhunter house and several others in the neighborhood remind us of more peaceful, slower-paced times of the Bluegrass.

Log Cabin

72

Todhunter House

View of Drive in the Fall

BOURBON COUNTY

JOHNSTON'S INN

CONSTRUCTED ORIGINALLY AS A STAGECOACH STOP FOR WEARY TRAVELERS, JOHNSTON'S Inn stands upon a rise of undulating Bluegrass land. One of the earliest coach taverns in Kentucky, it is as pleasant a sight today as it must have been to the travelers of yesteryear.

It is shown on John Filson's 1784 map of Kentucky as a two-story gabled building labeled "Capt. Johnston," which probably represented a log structure that was later replaced by the present brick building. According to Perrin's *History of Bourbon County*, there was a tavern here by 1790, and records show that the Johnstons paid for a tavern license in 1796. In the early 1800s, Fortescue Cuming, noted Irish-born traveler, recorded after having stayed at the inn that "Capt. Johnston" had a son and daughter living near him, a fine farm, "a quantity of last year's produce," and "luxuriant" wheat, corn, and tobacco fields.

Joseph Helm Clay purchased Johnston's Inn for his bride in 1832 and renamed it Rosedale, and the property was held by that family until 1956. It is said that in 1854 three of the Clay daughters died of cholera. At that time the house was painted white, and it remained so until recently when it was stripped to the original brick.

The brick structure has a two-story main block and a one-story wing which was the original "keeping" or "ordinary" room and bar. This wing is believed to predate 1800, with the two-story section built soon after. The latter has a recessed Greek Revival doorway. The building has been used as a residence since the nineteenth century and has had several alterations, but many of the original features are intact.

The present owners, who call the place Auberge, continue to cherish this unique Kentucky site and gave a large party honoring Johnston's Inn's long history. A song composed by the hostess for this occasion said about the house, "You're standing still upon the hill and may you ever be."

Johnston's Inn

Parlor

AUVERGNE

In 1904, Thomas A. Knight and Nancy Lewis Greene wrote in their book, *Country Estates of the Blue Grass*, "Auvergne . . . is one of the most noted [estates] in Kentucky. For years the residence has been one of the showplaces of Bourbon County, and has possibly been the scene of as many social functions as any country residence in Central Kentucky. In every respect it is a grand specimen of the architecture of the early part of the nineteenth century."

Auvergne was built ca. 1837 by Brutus J. Clay, second son of General Green Clay, whose home place was Clermont (later White Hall) in Madison County. The Bourbon property is said to have been a land grant to the general in 1783 by Patrick Henry and there Brutus and his wife, Amelia I. Field, settled in 1827, and he became one of the state's leading breeders of fine stock.

This house is an outstanding example of a transition between the Federal and Greek Revival periods. Another house in Bourbon County that is of this same transitional period and almost identical to Auvergne is Buknore on the Cane Ridge Road.

According to Walter Langsam, "Perhaps most striking [at Auvergne] . . . are the elliptical arches dividing the front half of the entrance hall from the stairhall at the rear; these are a Federal, not Greek, device, and they even have the concave Gothic console-like upper moldings associated with the late 18th century Federal style. The huge scale and support by convincingly Doric columns is utterly Grecian, however."

The unusual cast-iron porch over the main entrance is probably not original but has been documented as dating to 1861. Over the years, additions have been made to the wings, the last being added in the early part of this century. There is a remarkable number of outbuildings still standing at Auvergne, among them a smokehouse, slave houses, stable, carriage house, and others.

Architecturally and historically, Auvergne is very important in the annals of Bluegrass history, and today it belongs to the fourth generation of the family for whom it was built.

Outbuildings

78

Lion at Gate

Auvergne

KISER STATION

JOHN KISER, SR., CAME WITH HIS FAMILY TO KENTUCKY FROM MARYLAND VIA Virginia in 1780. For mutual protection, the Kisers and several other families built a fort located near where Cooper's Run flows into Stoner Creek. In 1785, Kiser built the original section of this house and settled down as the proprietor of a nearby grist mill, saw mill, and distillery. The Indian threat was still imminent, and in 1787 an attack killed four members of the Kiser family. This didn't drive them off, for a 1795 tax list shows that John Kiser had 1,000 acres of land and forty-seven slaves.

This early stone house is one of the most important in Bourbon County. It was the location of the second and third sessions of the Bourbon County Court in 1786, while the county was still a part of Virginia. According to Walter Langsam, "The original two-story stone portion of the dwelling faced north. On the hall-and-parlor plan, it has a particularly interesting flat Georgian mantel of a type rare in Kentucky. When a stone one-and-one-half-story wing was added early in the nineteenth century, the house was reoriented towards the creek and road to the east. This wing consists of a wide stairhall and large parlor, which features an elaborate mantel with wings above the paired colonettes. The mantel is flanked by large presses and above the shelf is a rare surviving wall-painting of a vase of roses with darting hummingbirds. Near the house are a stone smokehouse and an impressive log barn."

The Kiser family lived here for over 167 years, but the house was sold out of the family in 1952. The present owners have carefully maintained this architectural treasure, which so finely represents the days of the pioneer settlement of early Kentucky.

Kiser Station

Side View of House

81

MARCHMONT

As Central Kentuckians know, an abundance of Clays have been large landowners in Bourbon County for many years. To avoid confusion, they were often given nicknames. It was "Greybeard Sam," so called to distinguish him from six related Samuel Clays in the county, who built Marchmont about 1865.

In the book, *Horse World of the Bluegrass*, Dr. Mary Wharton says, "James E. Clay, son of 'Greybeard' Samuel Clay, was also an extensive landowner and after 1900 lived in Marchmont. Like his father he was a progressive agriculturist, raising hemp, corn, tobacco, cattle, sheep and hogs, but unlike his father he also raised many horses—trotters for both the road and the track. . . . He later added thoroughbreds to his operation and had a training track."

Architectural historian Walter Langsam has written that Marchmont is "one of the most splendid and intact of Italianate mansions in the Blue Grass. . . . Architecturally, Marchmont is remarkable, not only for its size and quality but also for its degree of intactness. . . . The interiors, also considerably intact, retain ornamental arches, rich plaster cornices, lush and variegated chandelier medallions, red Bohemian glass transoms, and important mantels."

Today Marchmont is occupied by the descendants of "Greybeard" Sam and has been incorporated into their Claiborne Farm, one of the most successful thoroughbred farms in the world. In their 1904 book, *Country Estates of the Blue Grass*, authors Knight and Greene say about Marchmont, "All the members of the family for several generations past were born and raised on the place. It is this feature that makes it absolutely ideal as a home, every tree, every building on the place, recalling the associations of a lifetime."

Marchmont

WYNDHURST

AIRY CASTLE WAS THE ORIGINAL NAME OF THE PLACE THAT WAS DESIGNED AND BUILT in 1872–73 by Confederate war veteran G. W. Bowen. George Bowen was a prosperous merchant and distiller, and his success in business is reflected in this impressive house. According to architectural historian Walter Langsam, "This great Italianate Second Empire country house . . . is one of the most remarkable and sensitively preserved dwellings of its period in the county—this includes the exterior, the interior and the context of outbuildings and farm landscapes."

The house is essentially a cube with a two-story ell. The Second Empire roof rises to a platform surrounded by wrought-iron cresting. Rainwater originally was fed into an attic tank to supply a second-story bathroom. The symmetrical plan of the house is offset with diversified gables, porches, window shapes, and other decorative features. The interior houses elaborate centerpieces and cornices and a forty-eight-foot hall running from the front door to back. Still intact are the two-story brick tenant houses with their hipped roofs and Italianate porches.

John LaRue and his wife Corrilla purchased Airy Castle in 1888 and changed its name to Wyndhurst, since they thought the original name too pretentious. John never enjoyed living at his imposing country estate, however, for he died the day he moved in. Nevertheless, his family has resided in this unique Bourbon County house for nearly one hundred years, which probably accounts for the almost unchanged condition of the residence and its surroundings.

Wyndhurst

Parlor

ESCONDIDA

THIS LARGE HOUSE WAS BUILT BY GENERAL GREEN CLAY, MOST LIKELY AS A WEDDING gift for his son, Sidney Payne Clay. The young Clay, a graduate of Princeton University, occupied the house until his death, and it stayed in the family until 1896.

Escondida (Spanish for "hideaway") is an outstanding example of the Federal style in Central Kentucky. The one-story main section is flanked by wings and is fronted by a Tuscan entrance porch with a lunette window in its pediment. A long porch on chamfered posts extends the rear of the house under the slope of the main roof.

Shortly after the turn of the century, Escondida was purchased by Robert Trimble Ford, a descendant of an early Bourbon County family, who had made a fortune in Texas. It was he who built the large stone barn. According to Walter Langsam, "This superb stone barn with its picturesque roof, including jerkin-headed or clipped-end gables and hipped-roof dormers, is attributed to the prominent New York City architectural firm of H. I. Copeland." Ford died in 1911, and the house was then lived in by tenants for several years.

In 1972, this important Kentucky house was sold to an old Bluegrass family, who painstakingly renovated it. Located on one of the highest spots in the county, Escondida proudly reigns again over the rolling landscape.

Stone Barn

Escondida

MOUNT LEBANON

Mount Lebanon is one of a group of important early stone buildings located in Bourbon County. It was illustrated in Lewis Collins' *Historical Sketches of Kentucky*, published in 1847, which provides some of the earliest views of Kentucky buildings. The engraving of Mount Lebanon shows it with a quaint rail fence along the road that ran in front of the house on a bluff overlooking Stoner Creek. The old road bed can still be seen today.

Constructed in 1786, it was the home of James Garrard, Kentucky's second governor, who was born in Stafford County, Virginia. He immigrated into Kentucky three years prior to building his house. The first county court of Bourbon County was held at Mount Lebanon in 1786 and for several years after that. James Garrard was elected governor of Kentucky in 1796 and remained in that post until 1804, having the distinction of being the only governor of this state to serve two consecutive terms.

Mount Lebanon is constructed of limestone cut and laid on the front to resemble the Flemish-bond brickwork pattern. The fine stonework of this house and several others in the county is attributed to the early builder John Metcalfe and his nephew Thomas "Stonehammer" Metcalf. The house still has many of the original pegged window frames and panelled interior jambs. There are fine stone jack arches with keystones over the front windows and door. During the Gothic Revival period, the homestead was remodeled. The eaves of the roof of the main block were extended and adorned with decorative bargeboards and supported with cast-iron brackets. A porch and front gable were added but later removed. During the remodeling, the interior was done more in the Greek Revival style. A stone wing was added in 1950.

Governor and Mrs. Garrard were the parents of twelve children, and Mount Lebanon was inherited by their daughter Margaret and her husband Isham Talbot. Talbot was a distinguished member of the Kentucky Senate, later becoming a United States senator. Today, almost 200 years after its construction, this house is lived in and the land around it worked by Governor Garrard's great-great-grandson, making him the fifth generation of the Garrard family to live at Mount Lebanon.

Mount Lebanon

Interior Showing Portrait of
Governor Garrard

HARKAWAY

THE MAIN BLOCK OF THIS DISTINGUISHED STONE RESIDENCE WAS CONSTRUCTED FOR Laban Shipp in the late 1780s. The small windows in the original large section of Harkaway are unusual, suggesting that this early pioneer fortified his residence against the Indian threats, which lasted into the next century.

In the side originally used as the front of the house, the fine dressed stone is laid in a Flemish-bond-like pattern, and the jackarches have dressed keystones. By 1817, a stone wing had been added, which displays a cornice of fine gougework. It was probably then that the main entrance of the house was reversed. It wasn't until the 1930s, however, when the house was purchased by descendants of the second owner, that other attractive additions were made, including a stone arcade in front of the kitchen, a one-story wing, and a garage attached to an early stone outbuilding.

Laban Shipp was a member of an aristocratic Virginia family, and when he settled in Bourbon County he became an important part of the early life of that area, running his mills on Stoner Creek and operating a distillery as early as 1800.

By 1817, the property was purchased by Abram Spears, another prominent early settler of the county. It is said that a member of the Spears family was among the first, if not the first, makers and distributors of "Bourbon" whiskey. By the mid-1800s, the property was sold out of the Spears family, but descendants bought it back in 1935, and it remains in the family today.

Harkaway

RUNNYMEDE

Runnymede is located on part of the large tract of land acquired by James Garrard, Sr., second governor of Kentucky. Governor Garrard's place, Mount Lebanon, is on the opposite side of Stoner Creek, which runs through the property.

The land was handed down to Charles Todd Garrard, and it was he who built this imposing structure in the 1830s and called it Locust Level. The house is Greek Revival in character, and if the 1830s construction date is correct, it is one of the earliest examples of this classical style in the area.

This fine two-story brick residence has colossal pilasters dominating the front and articulating the pedimental ends of the main block. The right wing and, probably, part of the large ell were raised to two stories after the Civil War. In the period before World War II, the north wing was greatly enlarged to provide a large living room. The interior walls are stone, and the exterior brick ones have pilasters relating to the main block. The round-arched windows of the north wing suggest an enclosed loggia.

After the Civil War, the place was sold to Colonel Ezekiel Field Clay, who bred shorthorns on his newly-named Runnymede. Although "Zeke" Clay was from the branch of the family that had mostly supported the Union, he was a staunch Confederate, who raised his own regiment and valiantly served the Southern cause in many important campaigns.

In the 1904 Knight and Greene publication, *Country Estates of the Blue Grass*, Runnymede is acclaimed not only as a stock farm, but as "a perfect type of the more prosperous Kentucky home." It remains so today, and is lived in by Colonel Clay's descendants, who operate a well-known thoroughbred horse farm.

Old Stone Barn

Runnymede

Parlor

THE LARCHES

WHEN THIS HOUSE WAS CONSTRUCTED FOR SENATOR GARRETT DAVIS, CA. 1840, IT was called Woodhome, but later owners named it The Larches for the two large trees that grow in front of the house.

Davis was born in 1801 in Mt. Sterling, Kentucky, and in 1823 began the practice of law in Paris. He had a prominent political career as he first served in the Kentucky House of Representatives and later in the U.S. Congress. He was strongly opposed to secession and supported the Union during the Civil War. After the war he was known for his attempts to moderate the force of Reconstruction. He was serving in the U.S. Senate at the time of his death in 1872.

Colonel George M. Edgar bought the house from Senator Davis' son in 1875. Reputed to be an "unreconstructed Rebel," Colonel Edgar established a school here that offered military instruction, and it appears from a photograph of that period that the uniforms were gray and similar to those worn by the Confederates. Although under new ownership, a school continued here well into the next decade, and it was probably around 1880 that a separate school house was built on the grounds.

This imposing Greek Revival house rests on a high basement through which extend the colossal Doric pilasters that frame the five front openings. The entrance, enclosed by a flat-roofed porch enhanced by four short Doric columns supporting a heavy entablature, gives this portico an unusually bold and heavy look. However, it is not out of scale with the mass of the brick house, which is much larger than it appears from the front.

In the early 1930s, The Larches was purchased by Mr. and Mrs. John Harris Clay, who sensitively renovated it. It remains today in that family, which for fifty years has steadfastly preserved the glories of this superb Greek Revival residence.

The Larches

Entrance Hall

THE GRANGE

ARCHITECTURAL HISTORIANS SEEM TO AGREE THE THE GRANGE IS ONE OF THE GREAT houses of the Bluegrass.

The exact date of construction is unknown, but it is believed to be in the latter part of the first quarter of the nineteenth-century. According to Walter Langsam, The Grange is "one of the finest Federal houses in Kentucky and has several unusual features. Its main five-bay central-hall plan block has a hipped roof, with two dormers across the front and the back; at the ends are pavilions, also with hipped roofs, and with gently curved fronts that are not reflected in the shape of the interior rooms, seeming to be intended purely for aesthetic affect, obviously at great expense; and large Palladian windows bent across these bows, with elaborate tracery of fan and sidelights echoing that of the wide round-arched entrance."

It is ironic that this sensitively designed structure was built for a notorious slave-trader, Edward Stone. J. Winston Coleman, Jr., in his book, *Slavery Times in Kentucky*, said that Stone imprisoned unruly slaves in the basement of his house, and when he had enough, he took them down river to sell at the Southern markets. Coleman also said that most Bluegrass residents abhorred slave traders. Stone announced in 1826 that he was giving it up to lead the life of a Kentucky planter, but he decided to make one more trip to sell a few surplus slaves. While anchored overnight in Western Kentucky en route to New Orleans, the slaves rose up against the traders and killed them. Ned Stone never returned to his fine Kentucky house.

There have been Kentucky gentlemen living there since the property was auctioned shortly after Stone's death. The place was known as Brentwood when occupied by the Brent family and was named The Grange by later owners, Mr. and Mrs. Sidney Clay. The present owners purchased the property in 1965 and continue to preserve this architectural gem.

HIDAWAY

Properly named, Hidaway is only a few blocks from downtown Paris, although the house is almost completely concealed on its large lot by foliage and landscaping.

Built between 1860 and 1870, the house is often described as the most characteristic large Gothic Revival residence in Bourbon County. According to Patrick Snadon, architectural historian, the composition of this house is closely related to one of A. J. Downing's designs, with a symmetrical facade, projecting arcade, and flanking verandas. Because of its close resemblance to Elley Villa, Lexington's finest Gothic Revival house, Hidaway has been attributed to the Lexington architect-builder John McMurtry, who also designed and built the Paris Cemetery gatehouse.

There is a difference of opinion about who had the house built, but according to Walter Langsam, it seems likely that it was constructed for W. W. Massie, who was living at Hidaway in 1877. Massie was a wealthy Paris merchant whose father, Jonathan Massie, an early Bourbon County settler, operated several tanneries as well as flour mills on Stoner Creek six miles from the city.

At W. W. Massie's death, his wife bequeathed this property to the city as a hospital. Fortunately, a larger property was acquired with funds from the sale of Hidaway, and the Gothic Revival retreat remained as a residence nestled in its picturesque setting.

XALAPA

XALAPA IS ONE OF THE LARGEST AND MOST ELABORATE FARM ESTATES IN THE
Bluegrass. The entire complex is unified by stone walls encompassing many
buildings, bridges, gardens, and horse facilities. The exceptionally long driveway
meanders through a park-like setting, and the avenues are bordered by a variety
of specimen trees.

The historic core of the property is the main house of Xalapa. It was built in
1827 for William T. Buckner, who came to Kentucky from Carolina County,
Virginia, in 1820 and settled in Bourbon County on the waters of Stoner and
Strode creeks. Buckner wrote to his contractor, "It is my settled determination to
have the house executed in the best manner, with inside chimneys and presses,
the two front rooms and passages to be in the best state, and the two back rooms
with wash and chair rails. The chimney pieces in the front rooms are to be the
handsomest, with those in the other rooms plain. The house is to have a
pediment on each side with circular door and window in front and rear so as to
have no difference in the appearance of the sides of the house."

The story-and-one-half Federal-style brick house has been enlarged over the
years, but the front and rear elevations are as Mr. Buckner instructed, with their
center gables enclosing Palladian windows over entrances with wide elliptical
fanlights.

The house remained in the Buckner family until 1897, the last of that clan
living there being Henry C. Buckner. It was he who gave it the name of Xalapa,
said to mean "happy land," after his return from service in the Mexican War. His
heirs sold the place to William Erskine Simms, and it later was owned by his son,
Edward Francis Simms, who had made his fortune in the Texas oil fields. Ed
Simms increased the acreage of the farm and developed the land to its present
superb form. He made the thoroughbred operation one of the most important in
America. Today, the beauty of Xalapa—the happy land—continues under the
guidance of this same family.

Xalapa

CLARK COUNTY

VINEWOOD

Clark County was well-known for its large stock farms and fine cattle herds, especially of the Shorthorn breed. Benjamin Groom was engaged in the importing and developing of this breed, and his success is reflected in Vinewood, the Italianate mansion that he had built ca. 1861.

Colonel Benjamin B. Groom imported many of his cattle from England. It is said that on a buying trip to that country, he was impressed with a certain manor house in the Italianate style, and from this he got the inspiration to build Vinewood. However, he suffered financial reverses in the panic of 1873 and soon afterward sold his cattle and his home and moved to Texas.

The *Survey of Historic Sites in Kentucky — Clark County* states, "The most stylistically sophisticated of the Italianate residences in Clark County is Vinewood. . . . The appearance of the Vinewood villa is one of asymmetrical complementary components which collect and meld on their hilltop site. In actuality, the main block of Vinewood is the familiar double-pile central-passage plan cleverly disguised by the dominating tower and the series of porches and bays." Among the unusual features of the house are the four sets of paired Italianate windows which make the Tuscan tower such an exceptional stylistic asset. Each pair of arched windows is separated by a Corinthian pilaster which balances a circular window. This entire group is surmounted by a molded sandstone arch.

Fortunately, Vinewood has changed very little in 122 years. Its overall effect on the traditional Clark County landscape must have been unique when the villa was built and even today it is one of the county's most distinguished houses.

HOLMHURST

Kathryn Owen, Clark County Historian, in her charming book, *Old Homes and Landmarks of Clark County, Kentucky*, describes Holmhurst by saying, "On a hilltop, dividing Strode and Hancock Creeks, stands the brick mansion built by Strauder Goff in 1840. It is located within a quarter of a mile of the site of Kinlock, an earlier Goff home, built by Thomas Jonas Goff, the father of Strauder Goff."

Thomas Goff came into Kentucky in 1785 with a hunting party led by Daniel Boone. He lived at Strode's Station until he acquired land on which he built a brick house in 1808. That house no longer stands. His son, who inherited more than a thousand acres, was able to build the large Greek Revival Holmhurst during a period of great prosperity when the family was well-known as successful breeders of Shorthorn cattle as well as Cotswold sheep.

Holmhurst is a five-bay, two-story brick structure with a large rear ell. It is a transition between the Federal and Greek Revival periods, being a massive Greek Revival adaptation of an earlier form. The front facade is laid in the Flemish-bond pattern, and the house is designed in the center-passage, single-pile plan. It is a house that adheres to the symmetrical order. Over the windows are unusual, heavy, one-piece wooden lintels with corner blocks and a keystone design. On the side of the rear ell, there is a one-story porch with arched doors to the interior. There are several very fine brick outbuildings remaining.

Now residing at Holmhurst and farming the same land is the fifth generation of the Goff family. They completed a renovation of the place in 1971 and continue to make improvements on a house that has been handed down carefully from generation to generation.

MAJOR JOHN MARTIN HOUSE

THIS EARLY HOUSE WAS BUILT CA. 1790 FOR MAJOR JOHN MARTIN, WHO WAS BORN IN Albermarle County, Virginia, and came to Kentucky in 1784, having received his rank at the Battle of Yorktown during the Revolutionary War. He eventually settled on Boone's Creek and built his house in this fertile section of what is now Clark County.

Major Martin soon reached prominence in this Kentucky outpost by being appointed the first sheriff of Clark County by the first governor of Kentucky, Isaac Shelby. Martin's son, Samuel, studied medicine at Transylvania University in Lexington. After practicing in Winchester, county seat of Clark County, he moved to the home place and became a country doctor. His office, in a small addition on the side of the house, was razed around 1900.

The house has been reoriented so that the present facade faces a later road. This late nineteenth-century change made little difference as the central entrances on the front and rear walls were identical. The one-and-one-half-story brick house has a double-pile, center-hall plan of its Tidewater predecessors, but its elongated details place it in the Federal period. In 1970, the present owners completed a rehabilitation of the house, keeping most of the original fabric in the main block and acquiring needed space by adding well-scaled wings to either side.

The Martins have been gone for many years, but their memory lives on, especially in the old family cemetery, only 500 feet from the house, which contains the graves of the major, his wife, and other family members.

Major John Martin House

Back Hall

POSSUMTROT

It is hard to realize that this large two-storied Greek Revival frame house of today was originally a dogtrot (or possumtrot) log house.

The *Survey of Historic Sites in Kentucky — Clark County* says, "Built c. 1825, it was raised to two stories and extensively altered by S. A. B. Woodford in 1849. The details added in that year include a pilastered door surrounded with an acanthus motif that was obviously derived from Minard Lafever's, *The Modern Builder's Guide*, published in several editions between 1833 and 1850. Other fine Greek details are the pedimented lintels, the three-part window sash, and the use of faceted corner blocks. . . . This still-traditional compound was associated with the latest trends of the Greek Revival by the application of exact pattern-book details."

Samuel A. B. Woodford was three years old in 1818 when he came to Kentucky with his father and grandfather. He later bought this log house, made the alterations in 1849, and lived on his farm for almost sixty years. During this time he was a cofounder of the Old Taylor Distillery, whose products were then manufactured on the banks of a nearby creek. After he died in 1906 at age 91, he was buried on the place.

Still the homeplace for Samuel Woodford's descendants, Possumtrot is an example of those sturdy, unpretentious Kentucky houses that were so often forged from earlier structures built in pioneer days.

STANLEY PLACE

THIS HOUSE WAS NAMED AFTER THE RICHMOND COUNTY, VIRGINIA, ESTATE KNOWN AS Stanley Hall, which was the home of the builder's great-grandfather. Stanley Place in Clark County, Kentucky, was built in 1858 for Stanley Foushee Tebbs on land that was inherited through his mother's family, the Hubbard Taylors of Springhill.

Stanley Place has an early nineteenth-century form embellished with Italianate details. It is a center-passage, double-pile house situated off the road, up a drive, past a pond, and in a grove of trees. The five-bay, gabled-roof house has wooden lintels over its windows and a quaint bracketed veranda on the front. There are brackets at the roofline and a large two-story rear wing.

The house is what most Kentuckians would call a nice country place with its comfortable house in a peaceful setting. This is surely how the builder's family has felt, for the sixth generation is now residing in this house, constructed prior to the Civil War.

HOLLY ROOD

AN ARCHITECTURAL RAMBLE THROUGH CLARK COUNTY WOULD BE INCOMPLETE without a visit to Holly Rood, the house built for James Clark, Kentucky's twelfth governor.

The publication *Survey of Historic Sites in Kentucky — Clark County* gives this description: "The first definite Federal house in Winchester was Holly Rood, which was built for Governor James Clark between 1813 and 1815. It was considerably more provincial in design than other notable Kentucky houses of the same period. . . . Even though it was probably the most elegant house in the immediate Winchester area when it was built, the plain wall surfaces, the simple box-like mass and the plain cornice of Holly Rood are elements of the basic simplicity which pervades this house. It relies for effect on the Palladian windows and fanlit doorways on both of the long facades and the delicacy of the relatively simple woodwork."

James Clark was born in Bedford County, Virginia, and came with his family to Kentucky at an early age. He went to Virginia to study law and returned to Kentucky in 1798 to open a law practice in Winchester. Clark had an illustrious career as a member of the Kentucky legislature, was elected to Congress in 1812 to succeed Henry Clay, and in 1836 was elected governor of Kentucky. He died in 1839 before completing his term.

Holly Rood once commanded a prominent place in the landscape, but over the years the town of Winchester grew up around it. Nevertheless, its future now looks brighter. Entered on the National Register of Historic Places in 1974, the house is now owned by the Winchester-Clark County Heritage Commission, which has restored it and opened Holly Rood to the public on a limited basis.

Holly Rood

Hall looking into Dining Room

CAVELAND

Nestled in what is referred to in the Bluegrass region as the hunt country is this lovely early Kentucky Federal-style house. Built for Richard Hickman in 1797, the house is situated about two hundred yards from the opening of a hillside limestone cave from which the house took its name.

Caveland is typical of those early two-story brick houses constructed by the pioneer families of the area. These sturdy houses were built to last, especially Caveland with its brick walls three feet thick. The front facade is laid up in the Flemish-bond pattern, and the three courses of protruding bricks between the first and second stories create the belt course. The pegged window frames are still in place, as is the simple but graceful four-light transom over the front entrance. It appears additions to the house came in stages, the first being a ca. 1840 one-story brick ell and later a Victorian-style porch. In 1978, after having fallen into a state of disrepair, Caveland was purchased and renovated by the present owner. The Victorian porch was removed and a stone terrace built along the front and one side of the house. The ell was enlarged, and a brick wing added.

General Richard Hickman was born in 1757 in Culpeper County, Virginia, and came into what is now Clark County, Kentucky, in 1784. He derived his title from having been appointed a major general in the Kentucky militia. Hickman was a member of the constitutional convention that framed the second Kentucky constitution in 1799, served in the Kentucky legislature for many years, and was elected lieutenant governor in 1812 on the ticket with Isaac Shelby. During his administration, the War of 1812 broke out, and there was a sharp disagreement between Hickman and Shelby as to which would go to the front and lead the Kentucky troops. The legislature directed Shelby to the war, and Richard Hickman remained at the capitol in Frankfort to act as governor.

Caveland is still serene in its setting well off the back-country lane that leads to it. On the place is the Hickman family graveyard, where the general and his wife Lydia are buried. Today there is much activity around the farm as the owner is the master of foxhounds of the nearby Iroquois Hunt, and during the season this fine old Kentucky house is a warming stop for the hunters and their friends on cool autumn days.

Caveland

SPRINGHILL

SPRINGHILL WAS BUILT IN 1792 BY HUBBARD TAYLOR. IT IS A WEATHER-BOARDED house of five bays with a central-passage plan and an early rear shed. The original roof design was gambrel, making it the only known example of this style in Central Kentucky. Also unusual are the glazed headers in the Flemish-bond brickwork of the two original chimneys. These features and the early construction date of this frame house make it a rare example of pioneer architecture in Kentucky.

The distinguished builder, Hubbard Taylor, was originally from Carolina County, Virginia. In 1780, after having served in the Revolutionary War, Taylor came to Kentucky as deputy surveyor for Kentucky County, Virginia. According to Taylor's papers, he was anxious to move to Kentucky but was unable to do so until 1790.

"Preparatory thereto," wrote Taylor, "I bought of Dr. Thomas Hinde 500 acres of his military tract in Kentucky—then Fayette County, brought out a part of my negroes, searched out the tract for 500 acres. . . . I also imployed [sic] a man to assist my hands in building some cabbins [sic]. . . . I also employed Thomas Minor, a nephew of my wife's, to take charge of my new intended home, and returned to Orange County, Virginia." Taylor with his wife and three children returned to Kentucky in the spring of 1790 and immediately began construction of the frame house that stands today.

Hubbard Taylor became a man of means and political importance in Kentucky. His descendants lived at Springhill until 1922, when it was sold to the present owner's mother. Set well off the road and surrounded by gently rolling, fertile land, this unusual Kentucky house adds to the versatility of architectural styles within the Bluegrass region.

Springhill

Hall

WOODFORD COUNTY

WELCOME HALL

ONE OF THE MOST CHERISHED EARLY KENTUCKY FARMS SURROUNDS THE FINE OLD house known by its warm and friendly name, Welcome Hall. Construction on the stone center section was started in 1789, three years before Kentucky became a state.

The original owner came into the region in the late 1780s, purchased the land, and proceeded with the building of his stone house. John Long soon became a successful farmer and, according to the 1810 census, was the owner of fifteen slaves. In 1816, the farm was sold to the Graddy family, which still resides there. William Lee Graddy had emigrated with his father from North Carolina in 1787 and was a bachelor when he bought Welcome Hall. The right wing was in existence by this time because it is known that Graddy lived in the ell three years before his marriage in 1819. He and his bride added the left brick wing and the two-story entrance porch ca. 1828.

The main mass is of hand-cut native limestone and has three bays, with a chimney on either end of the steeply pitched roof. The windows are small in relationship to the mass of the stone block, and the trim around the nine-over-six pane sash is simple in design. The lower windows have stone jack arches and keystones. The double portico, although added later, is plain in detail and blends with the sturdy character of the original section, especially with the addition of the two brick wings.

Welcome Hall retains much of its late eighteenth-century wood trim not only on the exterior but also on the interior. The central entrance leads directly into a living room much like an English "hall." This unusual room has the original paneled fireplace wall and a mantel with reeded pilasters. An interesting note is that the three sections of the house have second floors, none of which connect. "The fine hand-carved mantels and beautiful woodwork attest to the skill of the early Kentucky craftsman," states historian J. Winston Coleman.

Welcome Hall, set well off the road at the end of a long entrance drive, is one of the most attractive examples of early Kentucky architecture. The main block of hand-hewn stone with the well-proportioned brick wings marks the orderly growth of the house and together with its several surviving outbuildings presents a fine example of an early Kentucky estate.

Welcome Hall

English "Hall"

STONE CASTLE

IT IS NOT SURPRISING THAT THE NAME STONE CASTLE WAS GIVEN THIS EARLY
Kentucky house many years ago. Even though it is located well off the road,
those interested in early Kentucky architecture have usually found their way to
the picturesque setting which features this stone residence.

Ezra Hammon was born in 1774 in Virginia, married Hanna Farra, and
settled in Woodford County about 1800, and tradition has it that Stone Castle
was built then by John Farra for his sister and brother-in-law. At one time Ezra
Hammon owned as much as a thousand acres along the creek. By 1820, the farm
had been purchased by the Holloway family, whose heirs retained the house for
over seventy years. In 1970, the present owners decided to renovate the house
after it had been vacant for ten years. Before that it had been a tenant house.

Built in the Federal style, it is four bayed, has a story-and-one-half ell, and
22-inch thick walls. The stone of which it is constructed is often referred to as
"Kentucky River Marble," although quarried from nearby Clear Creek. The
two front doors are sheltered by the original porch which has chamfered posts,
but its original railings and later brackets are missing. The two rooms in the rear
ell have separate chimneys, which are placed off-center of the roof ridge line,
allowing the fireplaces to be centered in the two rooms. By doing this, the
builder provided higher roof joists, resulting in a taller ceiling on the adjoining
original side porch. These and other details show the care and craftsmanship that
blossomed in those early Bluegrass days.

Stone Castle is situated in a valley fairly close to Clear Creek with the field
between the creek and the house given over to growing burley tobacco. The
serene setting easily transports one back to those days when the brave
frontiersmen began the establishment of a Bluegrass culture carefully handed
down through many generations.

Stone Castle

WOODBURN

Woodburn, the Alexander estate in Woodford County, dates to 1790, when Robert Alexander of Scotland bought this tract of approximately 2,000 acres from the heirs of General Hugh Mercer, to whom it had been awarded for service in the French and Indian War. As a young man, Robert Alexander was Benjamin Franklin's private secretary when Franklin was in Paris to solicit French assistance for the American Revolution. The position previously had been held by Franklin's grandnephew, who married Robert Alexander's sister. Family tradition holds that it was Benjamin Franklin who first advised this young secretary to "Go west, young man."

Woodburn House was built in 1848 and became the home of Robert Aitchenson Alexander, Robert's oldest son. It was he who spent a great deal of his fortune in making Woodburn a fine estate and one of the greatest thoroughbred-breeding establishments in America. In describing Woodburn, architectural historian Bettye Lee Mastin said, "Remodeled and much-changed, the 26-room mansion today has a Greek Revival portico fronting the magnificent park it overlooks. To the right of the front hall are double libraries hung with chandeliers from Airdrie, the Scottish estate inherited by Robert. To the left are living and dining rooms and a cherry paneled music room, this last added in the 1890's." It was during Robert's tenure that land sold by his father was repurchased, and this, combined with other land, brought the size of the estate to 3,900 acres.

Under the ownership of R. A. Alexander, Woodburn excelled in the production of blooded stock, including cattle and sheep. According to *The Horse World of the Bluegrass*, "Then in 1853 he purchased his first thoroughbreds and began assembling top quality broodmares. In 1856, he purchased the famous Lexington for $15,000 and when someone questioned the wisdom of such an exorbitant price, he replied that he would sell a son of Lexington for more—and this he did. Lexington for a record sixteen years was America's leading sire and thus has the distinction of being the most successful sire in American Thoroughbred history."

The original land has been divided among heirs, but Woodburn House stands proudly today. It is the residence of sixth-generation Alexanders descended from the young Scotsman who heeded the advice of his mentor, Benjamin Franklin.

Woodburn

EDGEWOOD

THERE IS HARDLY ANOTHER HOUSE IN KENTUCKY THAT ILLUSTRATES SUCH A STRIKING transition between the Federal and Greek Revival architectural styles as Edgewood. Built in the late 1830s, probably by Joel DuPuy, a Huguenot settler who came into Woodford County in the 1780s from Pocahontas County, Virginia, the house and farm are more often associated with Colonel Willis Jones and his family, who purchased the place in 1846.

When looking at the front of this brick, story-and-one-half house, one is immediately struck by the Federal-style Palladian window located in the porch gable in contrast to the heavy square entrance, which is fully Grecian, with its fluted engaged columns, side pilasters, and entablature. Other exterior features, such as the end-gabled roof with paired chimneys, brick jack arches rather than plain lintels, and side galleries, all lean more heavily on the Federal period. The interior details also draw from both of these building styles.

Historically, Edgewood is most remembered for being the place where one of Kentucky's largest barbecues was held. In 1860, the visit of John J. Crittenden, former Kentucky governor, was the occasion for a barbecue during his travels throughout the state in the presidential campaign. About 25,000 people attended and heard Crittenden speak for two hours, his principal theme being the preservation of the Union. It seems ironic that a year later, there was another famous barbecue at Edgewood at which former vice president of the United States John C. Breckinridge and others delivered their farewell addresses before they left to join the Confederate forces.

The squire of Edgewood, Colonel Jones, was among those who spoke. He was killed in 1864 and buried in Richmond, Virginia. Mrs. Jones sent a note to President Lincoln requesting permission to pass through Union lines to visit the grave of her husband. Although his advisors urged him to deny the pass, Lincoln gave written permission, and Martha Jones made the trip to Richmond and brought back her husband's body to be buried in his home soil of Kentucky.

Edgewood

AIRY MOUNT

Located in Woodford County on the crest of a low, wide rise is Airy Mount, whose original portion was built in 1796. It is reputed to have been the second brick house constructed in Woodford County.

Airy Mount was built for Colonel William Henry Stanley Field, an officer in the Revolutionary War, who married his cousin, Sally Field, in Culpeper County, Virginia. They came to Central Kentucky prior to 1790 and took possession of his thousand-acre land grant. In 1799, Colonel Field was found guilty of murdering his wife, despite defense provided by Henry Clay, whose mother's farm adjoined Field's. Shortly after his execution, a female slave confessed to the crime.

Originally oriented toward Grier's Greek in the opposite direction from the present front entrance, the former front facade is laid up in Flemish-bond pattern with a beltcourse and water table. Around the 1840s a major addition was made to the house, so the interior now reflects the styles of both the Federal and Greek Revival periods. It was probably during this latter phase of construction that the front was reoriented when a door space under the main stairhall was enlarged to accommodate a double-door front entryway. In 1916, a one-story porch was added, visually incorporating the older and newer portions.

The house owes much of its interest to the murals in the hall and living room painted by Alfred Cohen. Cohen was born in France in the early 1800s and with two brothers settled in Woodford County sometime in the 1820s. He was principally known as a sign painter, although there are two other houses in the county known to have Cohen wall paintings. Included in the murals at Airy Mount are scenes of buildings, a village, rivers, bridges, a sailboat, and a steamboat called the *Henry Clay*. The paintings are in oil directly on the plaster. It is stated in the National Register description that "the overall effect of Cohen's murals is nothing short of delight. In part, this is achieved through the juxtaposition of simplified scenes beside complicated ones. His attention to detail is original and unique. The color schemes are pleasing, and the obvious inspiration and spontaneity add to the murals' charm."

Airy Mount

Stairway with Cohen Wall Painting

PLEASANT LAWN

PLEASANT LAWN WAS CONSTRUCTED IN 1829 FOR DANIEL JACKSON WILLIAMS ON LAND given to him by his father. The latter, Captain Williams, was descended from Sir William Williams, a Welsh baron, and from Roger Williams, the founder of Rhode Island. Captain Williams's wife, Mary Jackson Williams, was a close relative of President Andrew Jackson.

Daniel Jackson Williams was a surveyor, and tradition has it that he served as his own architect. Pleasant Lawn has a one-and-one-half story central section flanked by one-story wings of different widths. The surveyor-turned-architect was not as precise as one might expect, for the central section is served by an off-center arcade composed of nine arches that rest on circular piers. The central arch of the arcade is slightly larger than the rest and is not precisely aligned with the doorway. The Palladian window piercing the pediment is also off-center. The opposite or north façade is thought to have been the original front and has a pedimented porch supported by two brick columns. It also has a Palladian window in the pediment that displays a stone plaque at its peak, bearing the name of the builder and the date of construction.

Pleasant Lawn was owned by the Rogers family until 1964, although for many years prior to this the house either was vacant or was used as a tenant building. The new owners rehabilitated the house in spite of a fire that gutted the interior of the center section. The woodwork was carefully reproduced by expert craftsmen and the Alfred Cohen murals faithfully copied from color photographs, repainted onto canvas and attached to the walls. Today Pleasant Lawn is lived in by a prominent Texas horseman and his family, and it has regained its stature as one of the early unique and charming houses of the Bluegrass.

Pleasant Lawn

Parlor

OLD MOSS HOUSE

IT APPEARS THAT THE MOSS FAMILY OWNED THIS HOUSE AND FARM FOR A SHORTER period than other owners, but in Woodford County it is usually referred to as either Moss Side or just the Old Moss House.

It should be known as the Watkins House, for it was built for Henry Watkins, an early Woodford County settler. He purchased the property in 1793 from his brother John, who had taken up a thousand-acre grant on the waters of Grier's Creek. Back in Virginia, the brothers John and Henry Watkins had married sisters, Mary and Elizabeth Hudson. The latter was the widow of the Reverend John Clay and the mother of Henry Clay. When the Watkinses came to Kentucky, Henry remained in Richmond, working as a law clerk. The young lawyer came to Lexington in 1797 and made many trips to Woodford County to visit his mother. Mrs. Watkins and her husband kept a tavern in the village of Versailles, the first in town it is said. According to William Railey in his *History of Woodford County*, the inn was "quite a celebrated hostelry a century ago, and the rendezvous of great lawyers, pedagogues and statesmen of the day."

It was around 1820 that the Watkinses gave up the tavern, built their house, and settled on their farm. The house is finely executed as a well-proportioned brick structure in the Federal style. The two-story, four-bay house is laid up in the Flemish-bond pattern. There is a one-and-one-half-story brick wing also in Flemish-bond, which appears to have been added shortly after the main block. The one-room stone kitchen was originally connected to the wing by a dogtrot which is now enclosed. The double-entrance doors are sheltered by a one-story pedimented porch.

This early Bluegrass farm complex is charming in its undisturbed setting. As Elizabeth Simpson said in her 1930s publication, *The Enchanted Bluegrass*, "A crumbling stone wall encloses a meadow between the yard and the road, and down in the ravine is the little spring house where Henry Clay took milk and melons to be chilled on scorching summer days."

Old Moss House

PISGAH CHURCH

THE PISGAH PRESBYTERIAN CHURCH WAS ORGANIZED IN 1784 SOON AFTER THIS PART of Woodford County was settled by a group from Virginia who were mainly Scottish and Irish Presbyterian. The first church was a log structure, which was razed in 1812 and replaced by the present stone building. The Kentucky Academy stone building located directly behind the church was also constructed in 1812 and now serves as the Sunday school.

Originally, the stone church building was simpler than it is now. In the 1860s, it was remodeled with Gothic-style windows and a lacy bargeboard was added to the front gable. The walls are of randomly-laid local stone, except around the openings and at the corners, where quoins are suggested by regular blocks. The windows were filled with stained glass in 1888. The Kentucky Academy building also received Gothic-style windows around the turn of the century, and in 1954 a lateral section was added at the rear.

The graveyard adjoining the church building is in one of the most serene, unspoiled settings in Kentucky. Surrounded by a stone fence and nestled among ancient trees, it creates a strikingly beautiful scene. The cemetery is the burial site of pioneer settlers and many early members of the congregation, including five Revolutionary War soldiers.

The religious and social life of the Pisgah community has maintained a continuous link with the church, and the spacious and well-kept grounds provide recreational facilities. Tennis was introduced there in the 1890s, and one of the highlights of the area is still the annual Pisgah Tennis Tournament, at which the spectator watches a fine display of the sport played against the background of the majestic, rolling Bluegrass countryside.

Pisgah Church

View from Cemetery

HIGHLAND PLACE

SINCE ITS CONSTRUCTION IN 1862, HIGHLAND PLACE HAS BEEN THE HOME OF THE Garrett family. William Garrett came into Kentucky from Virginia in the 1700s, eventually settling in Woodford County. His grandson, Robert Garrett, built the present house on land owned by the family since 1782 and made great improvements to the farm.

Approaching Highland Place through the stone gates, one is immediately impressed by its Greek Revival appearance. Built during the period of "borrowed styles," the house has Greek Revival massing, Gothic Revival details both inside and out, and some Italianate elements, principally the brackets under the eaves. Each bracket has an acorn finial. The chimneys are set in the interior walls. Their shafts separate at the roof line and reunite at the cap, giving another very Gothic element to the total design. The front door is Greek Revival in style with the elaborate machine-turned consoles, which were popular in the Bluegrass area during this period. As this scroll design element had no function, it was used only for its visual delight.

The Garretts of Highland Place were known for their stock breeding, and at one period during the last century the farm was called "the headquarters of the saddle horse in Kentucky." It was here that many good saddle horses had their home, including Black Squirrel and Montrose, both buried on the place. Equally noteworthy was the flock of registered Shropshire sheep, which was considered one of the finest and largest in the South.

In more recent years, Highland Place has been best known for its extensive orchards. The house and the land are still being cared for by the descendants of those who first settled this tract over 200 years ago.

Highland Place

JACK JOUETT HOUSE

THE JACK JOUETT HOUSE IS A STORY-AND-ONE-HALF EARLY BRICK STRUCTURE BUILT in front of a one-story stone structure that now serves as the rear ell. The stone portion is believed to have been built as early as the late 1780s.

Captain Jack Jouett built the brick house in the late 1790s after moving to Woodford County. The small Federal-style cottage is charming in its simplicity and is a good example of early Kentucky craftsmanship. The brick is laid in Flemish-bond and the gabled porch on the front is supported by four small wooden chamfered posts. The porch pediment has no ornamentation, but the three gabled sides are enhanced by a decorative scallop-shaped cornice on the lower edge. Eventually, a dogtrot was built between the stone cabin and the house and was later enclosed to make an additional room. The house retains its simple Federal woodwork.

As described in the National Register nomination, "Jack Jouett is recorded in the annals of history because of a daring all-night ride of 40 miles on June 3, 1781, to save Governor Thomas Jefferson and members of the Virginia Legislature at Charlottesville from capture by the British, led by Colonel Banastre Tarleton. Because of Jouett's daring ride over rough roads and backwoods wilderness, from the Cuckoo Tavern 12 miles east of Louisa Court House, to Jefferson's Monticello, the Virginia Governor and members of his Legislature were saved at a time when their capture would have meant serious consequences for the already beleaguered colonies." His warnings, first to Jefferson at his farm and then to the assembly members who were meeting in Charlottesville, gave them time to escape their would-be captors. Jouett was rewarded by the Virginia assembly with a fine sword and a brace of pistols. Today many historians feel Jouett's ride more important than although not as well known as that of Paul Revere. It saved a large number of more influential men, and the ride was much longer and over much rougher terrain, but has never been accorded its proper place in American history.

It was not long after his wild ride that Jouett and his wife, Sally Robards, settled in Kentucky. They became the parents of twelve children, one of whom was Matthew Harris Jouett, Kentucky's most distinguished portrait painter. This home of two famous Americans is owned by Woodford County and has recently been restored by the Woodford County Heritage Committee, Inc. It is opened on a limited basis to the public.

Jack Jouett House

Parlor

135

MUNDAY'S LANDING

MUNDAY'S LANDING WAS A WELL-KNOWN TAVERN AND HOTEL THAT SERVED RIVER travelers and others on the Lexington-Harrodsburg turnpike. It was one of the busiest landings on the Kentucky River because it was located near the beginning of the river's navigation system and because a ferry crossed the river in front of the house. Many of the products shipped from the Bluegrass area were sent to Munday's Landing. The steamboats carried goods such as hempen bagging, bale rope, wheat flour, corn, grain, and meats from the Bluegrass to the deep South.

It is known that the present house came into existence in 1847, but it has not been determined whether it was a totally new structure or additions added on to an earlier one. According to Bettye Lee Mastin, authority on Bluegrass architecture, "Greek Revival door frames reinforce the idea of an 1847 date, but there are details that make the house seem either transitional—built in the period between Federal and Greek Revival—or an earlier house on which Greek Revival details were superimposed. Its Federal elements include chair railing, a staircase with a closed stringer, ash floorboards (later builders usually made them with poplar) and Carpenter locks."

Devoid of surface embellishment, this massive, austere clapboard house reveals the elementary craftsmanship of a provincial builder. Basically rectilinear, the gable-roofed structure breaks form with the inclusion of a giant front portico and double-level porch overlooking the river to the west.

Thomas Munday settled here sometime before 1800. He built a log house overlooking the river, operated a boatyard, and in 1817, purchased the ferry below his house. His son Jeremiah built the present hotel and tavern, which operated as such until around the turn of the century. Gone are the days of commercial traffic on this part of the Kentucky River, but Munday's Landing stands prominently on the hill, reminding us of those steamboat days of the Bluegrass.

Munday's Landing

Scott County

HARVEY C. GRAVES HOUSE

THIS HANDSOME 1859 GREEK REVIVAL HOUSE REPRESENTS A LATE VERSION OF THAT style in the Bluegrass. Its bracketed roofline and pediment reflect the romantic style of architecture that had recently been introduced into Central Kentucky.

Harvey C. Graves was the son of Colonel John Graves, who had come into Kentucky in 1786 and who was known for his active role in Indian fighting and helping newcomers who were settling in the wilderness. Harvey successfully pursued the fields of agriculture, finance, religion, and manufacturing. His biography in 1879 said, "Few men have been more useful or more widely esteemed; and by an active, successful, public-spirited, unselfish life, he has made the world better for having lived in it."

He made Main Street in Georgetown more attractive when he built this two-room-deep house with its triple windows under stone lintels. The front property line is outlined by a handsome cast-iron fence with the same pattern reflected in the iron-rail balcony over the front door.

The house was lived in by Graves's daughter and son-in-law, Mr. and Mrs. John Berkley, who sold the place in 1907. After several owners, it was sold in 1961 to Georgetown College to serve as the president's residence. This is a fitting use, as Harvey Graves was one of the founders of the college and served a number of years as a trustee.

SHROPSHIRE HOUSE

On Main Street in Georgetown, Kentucky, only a few doors from the downtown commercial area, is this charming townhouse. The National Register form states, "Called perhaps the most interesting house in Georgetown by architectural historian Rexford Newcomb, Shropshire House is a one and a half story brick house revealing some hints of its 1814 construction, but appearing typically of the period of its rebuilding or extensive remodelling during the early Greek Revival era. The facade reveals a long four bay facade pierced by three triple windows and a fanlight doorway with sidelights sheltered by a one story Ionic portico with pedimented entablature. . . . A Greek key design ornaments the fanlight door, and the pediment and cornice are trimmed with small dentils."

The little girl who lived at Shropshire House with her parents, Robert J. and Emily Flournoy Ward, from 1828 to 1833 received great notoriety during her lifetime. *A History of Scott County* by Ann Bolton Bevins says, "At this house resided little Sallie Ward for the first six years of her life. Her future would mark her, in the words of Dr. Thomas Clark, as 'born to be a princess.' Artist George Peter Alexander Healy included a lifesize portrait of her among three portraits of the beauties of Europe and declared her 'the most exquisite woman that he had ever painted.'

Sallie, by the time she was eighteen, was known in print as 'the belle of the state.' At twenty-one in 1848, she married Boston scion T. Bigelow Lawrence and set out to awaken Boston. Being the first 'bloomer girl' of that city, she shocked the city also by appearing on the street in slippers and with bare ankles. She succeeded in establishing four marriages prior to her death in 1896."

AUDUBON

ACCORDING TO ANN BOLTON BEVINS, AUTHORITY ON SCOTT COUNTY ARCHITECTURE, the stone section of the ell that was the original house could date as early as the 1790s. It was built by pioneer James Stephenson, who sold 130 acres and his stone house, known as Cedar Hill, to Charles B. Lewis in 1829 for $21 an acre. Lewis added a one-and-one-half-story brick kitchen wing to the gable end of the stone house about 1840, and on the other end he erected a massive, two-story Greek Revival brick house.

This Greek Revival section is five bays in width with an unusually heavy distyle pedimented portico similar to a neighboring house, Glencrest. In spite of its obvious Greek Revival portico and entrance, Audubon has brick jack arches over its openings, a shallow cornice, and window sizes reflecting an earlier period. These contrasts in style add to the interest of this well-known Scott County structure.

Charles Lewis was a contractor and builder and one of the pioneers of railway transportation in Central Kentucky; he supervised the construction by the Lexington and Ohio Railroad Company of the tracks between Lexington and Frankfort. A charter for this company was approved by the Kentucky legislature in 1830, making it one of the first in the United States. The construction was unique, for the tracks were made of long, narrow blocks of limestone laid end-to-end in which holes were drilled. Thin strips of iron were then spiked to the stone blocks.

Audubon remained in the Lewis family until 1932. The present owners diligently maintain this interesting, eclectic house, which stands near the tracks that were so important to the earlier owner and opened up Kentucky's first railroad.

Audubon

Spring House

143

VILEY HOUSE

Located well off one of the picturesque county roads outside of Georgetown, , this Greek Revival house was built for the family of one of Scott County's early settlers.

George Viley and his family came into Kentucky from Maryland in 1795 and settled on this farm the next year. The farm they left was known as Wolf Cow, and there they had raised thoroughbred horses. They continued this pursuit in Kentucky and were among the first to introduce thoroughbreds into the area. There were six Viley children who immigrated into Kentucky with their parents, and six more were later born there. The Viley children married well, and this pioneer family's blood can be found in many of the prominent early Bluegrass gentry.

Today, the farm is known as Groverland and sits gracefully on a slight rise where the owners may look over the countryside through Greek Revival triple windows. The front door is typical of that style and is sheltered by a well-proportioned portico. The present owners had properly scaled matching wings added to the main block of the house. To the rear is a fine small brick structure that sits on a high stone basement. This building is earlier than the main house, although a portico and heavy cornice were added to keep it in harmony. There are several other farm outbuildings that add charm to the setting of Groverland.

Brick Outbuilding

Viley House

NEWTON CRAIG HOUSE

Several miles outside of Georgetown, facing one of the main roads, is a fanciful Italianate villa-style house built ca. 1870 by one of Scott County's most colorful citizens.

Newton Craig, as keeper of the Kentucky penitentiary from 1843 to 1855, held one of the most lucrative political positions in the commonwealth. It is presumed that during this period the original house, now the back wing of the present house, was constructed by prison labor. This brick ell has four bays and was built in the Greek Revival mode. It probably wasn't until 1871, after Craig had won his fight with the Kentucky legislature over funds owed him for service as head of the penitentiary, that he built his noble villa. The imposing central tower is reached by its own winding stairway, designed as a miniature of the main stairway. According to Ann Bolton Bevins, "It is definitely one house that still speaks with the personality of its builder, with its elegance of detail spelled out with cast iron hoodmolds, balconies and ash-floored porch as well as interior floors."

Still standing near the house are two interesting outbuildings that harken back to the early days of Kentucky prisons. One is a small gabled-roof structure used as a holding pen for Craig's prisoners. The other is a three-story winery, used today as a barn but originally to house Craig's winemaking operation. The grapes on his many acres of vineyards were all tended by prison labor. In later years Newton Craig became quite an authority on grape culture and winemaking in addition to founding the Kentucky Beekeepers Association.

As Mrs. Bevins says, "The vineyards which covered the fields for miles around Craig's 360 acres have long disappeared, and the whipping post used for disciplining miscreant convicts is but a legend"; nevertheless, this colorful Kentuckian left a charming legacy in his Italianate villa set in the Bluegrass countryside.

Newton Craig House

Winery

KENSTON

WHEN KINZEA STONE BUILT HIS QUEEN ANNE-STYLE MANSION UP THE HILL FROM downtown Georgetown in 1892, he spared no expense. According to Mrs. Bevins in *A History of Scott County As Told by Selected Buildings*, "Ornamental use of stone, stained glass, and a variety of finely polished and elegantly carved woods helped to complete the architectural picture of the brick castle-like house set between its two neighbors of stone. . . . The house was the work of architects Frank L. and Edwin W. Smith, who worked as Smith Brothers of Lexington. Their specifications called for Akron vitrified pressed brick of a cherry-red color, brown-stained mortar, a curved front constructed of eight-inch-radius brick and all wood to be protected by brick. The tower finial was to be gilded with gold leaf." Not only exterior but interior details were the best quality, including Tiffany-glass windows, marble, and such woods as oak, sycamore, and cherry.

Kinzea Stone, originally from Bourbon County, had an obvious talent for business and during the latter quarter of the nineteenth century gained success in grocery, tobacco, whiskey, and real-estate enterprises. Stone also excelled in the world of thoroughbred horses and in 1891 won the Kentucky Derby with his horse Kingman, ridden by Isaac Murphy.

However, the real tribute to Kinzea Stone is his massive residence, Kenston. Today his descendants live with the family furnishings in rooms with original wall coverings, overlooking this small Central Kentucky town.

Kenston

Front Hall

149

CLIFTON

Built ca. 1842, this Federal-style house with its Greek Revival details occupies one of the most pleasant settings in Scott County. On a hill overlooking McConnell's Run and the site of Herndon's Station (1790), Clifton was the home of Leonidas Johnson and his wife Irene.

The plans were drawn by Colonel Johnson, and the house was built for his bride on land that had been settled by her grandfather in the 1790s. The Ionic doorway set in antis is protected by a one-story portico supported by four slender Ionic columns. The delicate detail of the porch entablature is repeated on the front cornice. In the late nineteenth century, the front dormer windows were added, as well as a wing on the east end of the house. This wing was removed when the house was restored in the late 1930s.

Leonidas Johnson was the son of Colonel James Johnson, who served in the United States Congress and who was considered one of the wealthiest men in Kentucky before his death in 1826. His uncle, Richard M. Johnson, was a U.S. senator and later vice president of the United States under Martin Van Buren. In 1915 descendants of Leonidas Johnson received from the United States government a sum of more than $37,000 as payment for 461 hogsheads of sugar taken by the Union Army from Johnson's Louisiana plantation during the Civil War. According to Mrs. Bevins, "The claim was granted on grounds that Johnson 'had remained loyal to the Union during the war.' A member of an intensely loyal Confederate family, Johnson stayed home and managed the agricultural interests while other members of the family fought the war."

HUBBARD A. VARNON HOUSE

THIS BOARD-AND-BATTEN GOTHIC REVIVAL RESIDENCE IS A GOOD EXAMPLE OF THAT style. Like so many houses originally built on farms near town, it now is surrounded by other houses on a city street.

Built ca. 1850 for Hubbard A. Varnon on his small farm, its design is attributed to the well-known Lexington architect and builder John McMurtry. Patrick Snadon, architectural historian, wrote in his master's thesis that "the house sits upon a massive stone foundation, and even the interior walls are supported in this manner. In place of the usual bargeboards, it has Italianate style brackets under the overhanding eaves. This is a happy substitution as the angle of the brackets runs parallel with the slope of the eaves and seems a more structural, functional solution than the 'fussier' look of the high ornamental bargeboards."

The house is an L plan, with a symmetrical facade and a central hall flanked by parlor and dining room. The hall contains a fine spiral staircase and the interior detail is Greek Revival, with the exception of some elaborate Victorian plasterwork and cast-iron. The front facade has an elaborately-detailed porch supported by octagonal piers and lined with a trim of Tudor arches with cut-out trefoil designs.

In 1889 the owners of a widely-heralded twine factory bought the house and its acreage in order to erect their industrial buildings on the land. Commercially, this was a boon to the city of Georgetown, not only because of the number of people employed but also because the factory provided an outlet for the hemp that was an important Central Kentucky crop. The business failed, the plant was torn down, and the land subdivided, resulting in this Carpenter Gothic residence being located in the middle of an early twentieth-century neighborhood.

HAWKINS HOUSE

THE HAWKINS HOUSE IS CONSIDERED BY MANY TO BE ONE OF THE MOST IMPORTANT landmarks in Georgetown. It is an interesting structure, having been built in three sections at three different times. The west wing was built in the late 1790s by John Hawkins, the east wing by Thomas Hawkins around 1815, and the two-story main block of the house ca. 1820.

The early west wing has its chimney and stairway standing independent of the adjoining main block. Its woodwork is plainer than the later east wing, which displays reeded recesses and some reeding on the chair rail and mantel. Ann Bolton Bevins says, "One is tempted to conclude that the two two-bay wings stood alone at first and were later joined by the main block of the house, or that the central area was initially occupied by a log structure." The Greek Revival portico was probably put on the house at the time the upstairs room was completed.

The National Register description of the Hawkins House states that this building is doubly significant in the history of the region. Its location is the site of an early rope walk and bagging factory. Secondly, the Hawkins House was the first building to be owned by the founders of Georgetown College, the earliest Baptist College west of the Appalachians. At one time, it was used as the home of the college president and later as a men's dormitory.

In spite of its varied uses, this early Kentucky house has held up well and benefited from a sensitive rehabilitation in the 1950s. It faces north, looking across the campus of Georgetown College, both being important parts of the history of this Kentucky town.

Hawkins House

Parlor

WARD HALL

REXFORD NEWCOMB, ARCHITECTURAL HISTORIAN, CALLED WARD HALL "THE MOST fabulous house in Central Kentucky." Built for Junius Ward in 1856, the house was constructed for the lavish price, for those times, of $50,000.

There is probably no other house in the Bluegrass that represents the height of the Greek Revival period more elegantly. Built on the Corinthian order, its two-story tetra-style portico has columns forty feet high that support a deep, pedimented entablature. Pilasters with Corinthian capitals ornament all four sides of the house, which is seventy-five feet square. The interior carries out the attention to details with plaster cornices rich with decorations of egg-and-dart and bead-and-reel patterns and anthemion blossoms. The woodwork is rubbed walnut, and a gracious winding staircase ascends to the third floor.

It was Junius Ward's father, General William, who laid the groundwork for the fortunes that his sons amassed. General Ward was an early Indian agent and secured for his family choice plantations along the Mississippi River. Junius Ward used his Kentucky estate as his summer home, making the deep South his permanent residence. His brother Robert was reputed to be the wealthiest man in Kentucky, and it was his beautiful daughter, Sallie, the most noted belle of the South, who was frequently guest of honor at the grand balls at Ward Hall.

After the Civil War, Junius Ward found his fortune gone. He was forced to sell Ward Hall, which was advertised at the time of the sale as the "finest country residence in this section of the country." A later owner, Colonel Milton Hamilton, offered the house with 250 acres, plus $50,000, to the Kentucky Legislature should it agree to use the property for the state capitol.

Ward Hall has been owned by several families over the years. The latest owners have recently refurbished it and have it open on a limited basis as a house museum. It has attracted many admirers but none were more inspired than the builder's nephew who wrote that Ward Hall was "the finest place in Kentucky at that time, a veritable palace surrounded by a fairy garden."

Ward Hall

View of Parlors from Dining Room

JESSAMINE COUNTY

HEART'S EASE

THIS IMPOSING GREEK REVIVAL RESIDENCE, CALLED HEART'S EASE FROM ITS EARLIEST days, was built in the mid-nineteenth century for James H. O'Neal. In 1860, the house and farm were purchased by William Simpson who was the son of Peter Simpson, who had come to America from Ireland, settled in Pennsylvania, fought in the Revolutionary War, and moved to Kentucky around 1780. William's wife was Amanda Cleveland Simpson, who, according to family tradition, wore heavily starched dresses and had a penchant for diamonds. When she died, she left her six sons that enviable combination—land and diamonds.

According to the *Survey of Historic Sites in Kentucky—Jessamine County*, "Heart's Ease, the O'Neal-Simpson House, has many of the most popular features of Jessamine County's version of the grand Greek Revival house. The two-story, five-bay block has a central passage plan that is supplemented by a two-story ell equipped with galleries on both sides. The chief exterior feature is the broad portico that extends across the three central bays of the main facade. The portico is supported by square brick piers and is interrupted on the second-floor level with a balcony. Both because of its imposing dimensions and proportions and its location on a major highway, Heart's Ease is one of the best-known Greek Revival structures in the county." A remodeling in the 1880s raised the rear wing to two stories, and in 1926, the original two-columned porch was altered to the present impressive portico with four brick piers. Several years ago, Heart's Ease was sold out of the Simpson family, the house rehabilitated and the name changed to Spring Mint Farm.

PLEASANT GROVE

THIS PICTURESQUE GREEK REVIVAL-STYLE HOUSE IS NESTLED IN A GROVE OF OLD BLUE ash and tulip poplar trees not far off the Keene-Troy Pike in Jessamine County. The house was constructed in 1846 for Whitfield Hayden, whose father, John Hayden, had come into this part of Kentucky in 1781 from Spottsylvania County, Virginia, heading one of the earliest families to settle here.

Pleasant Grove is unique in that its Greek Revival exterior houses an interior motif reflecting the Gothic Revival period. According to the *Survey of Historic Sites in Kentucky—Jessamine County*, "The chief exterior feature is the carefully designed two-story portico, which is much less common in the county than monumental porticoes. The delightful interior moldings consist of octagonal posts connected above the openings by horizontal strips of crenellation." It is known that the construction of the house was done by two mid-nineteenth-century builders named Andrew Muldrow Young and Ephraim January Young. How much of the design was theirs and how much that of the owner is not known, but framed and hanging in the house today is the original sketch of the floor plan by the builders. It is rare to find this evidence of early architects or builders, although it is believed that the Youngs built several houses in that section of the county.

Pleasant Grove remained in the Hayden family until 1905. In 1945, the present owner's grandmother purchased the property, and he and his wife have lived in and nurtured this fine old Kentucky residence. Although it has been in the present family for only about forty years, the master of Pleasant Grove is a descendant of the original builders, Ephraim and Andrew Young.

JAMES MARTIN HOUSE

ONE OF JESSAMINE COUNTY'S EARLIEST BRICK HOUSES IS THIS FINE TWO-AND-ONE-HALF-story residence built for James Martin probably about the end of the 1700s. Records show that Martin and his wife owned this land in 1791.

James Martin was the son of Benjamin Martin of Spottsylvania County, Virginia. He fought in the Revolutionary War and came into Kentucky in the 1780s. He must have been a young soldier in that war, for records show that when he died in 1845, he was eighty-seven years of age. According to historian Bettye Lee Mastin, in the year before his death, Martin legally declared that "finding myself unable and unwilling from my age to manage my farm and Negroes think it best upon due reflection to hand over the whole concern to my son Lewis G. Martin." In return, his son promised to "do all he can for the comfort and happiness of his father, furnish him in all the comforts of life that his age and situation required." The elder Martin died the next year and was buried in the orchard with a tombstone inscribed, "Here lies an old soldier of '76."

The *Survey of Historic Sites in Kentucky—Jessamine County* says, "The James G. Martin House is one of the most architecturally significant of Jessamine County's early brick houses, because of the richness of the interior and the house's fine state of preservation. The plan is hall and parlor, and the main facade consists of four bays rather than the usual five found in other brick houses of the period. The two floors are divided on the exterior by a belt course and the brickwork, as one would expect, is Flemish bond with jack arches. The mantels, chair rails, and window and door reveals are unusually rich, suggesting authorship of a master carpenter with an appreciation for delicacy, the chief aesthetic goal of Federal woodwork. There are two enclosed corner staircases, one in the main block and the other in the rather short, two-story ell." During the 1958 renovation of the house, the kitchen wing had to be razed, but it was rebuilt with the old brick. Otherwise, there have been few changes to the structure, except that the front entryway has recently been covered with a small porch.

This Federal-style house remained in the Martin family until the 1860s when it was sold to an Irishman named Edmund Kenney. It was from his heirs that the present owner's parents bought the place in 1958. It is well maintained and peaceful in its tranquil setting where the "old soldier of '76" had brought his family to settle in those early days of Kentucky.

James Martin House

HERVEY SCOTT HOUSE

SOMETIME AROUND 1840, THIS MAJESTIC GREEK REVIVAL RESIDENCE WAS CONSTRUCTED in this part of Jessamine County, which is close to the Kentucky River. Hervey Scott, for whom the house was built, was the son of one of the area's earliest settlers, John Scott.

John Scott, an Irish Presbyterian, immigrated to America in 1775 and into Kentucky via Virginia in the 1780s. Tradition says that he came with all his worldly goods wrapped in a red rag tied on a stick and with two shillings and nine pence in his pocket. From that time on, he signed all instruments of writing with "John 2/9 Scott" and was known in the region as 2/9 Scott. He had fought with General Wayne in the Indian wars and had come to Kentucky to settle on a land grant in the southern part of Jessamine County. He increased his holdings to several thousand acres and prospered on his fertile Kentucky land. He shipped goods downriver to New Orleans by flatboat and walked back to Kentucky on the Natchez Trace. Scott represented his county in the State legislature, and he built a fine stone house called Stoney Lonesome. Upon his death, he was able to leave all four of his children large tracts of land.

The house his son Hervey had built would have made old 2/9 Scott proud. As described in the *Survey of Historic Sites in Kentucky—Jessamine County*, "The chief glory of this mid-nineteenth century Greek Revival house is the portico, and eccentric interpretation of the Greek Doric order. The entablature shows acquaintance with patternbooks of the time, but the unfluted brick columns are far more tapered than the subtleties of entasis, an ancient technique of distorting the shape and position of architectural members for the sake of perceived regularity and perfection, would require. As in most Greek Revival houses of the Bluegrass, the portico does not extend across the full front."

As there are apparently no descendants of 2/9 Scott left on the many acres he acquired in the early days of Jessamine County, this grand house, built by his son, stands as one of the few tangible traces of this energetic pioneer family.

Hervey Scott House

THE GRANT KNIGHT HOUSE

THE BLUEGRASS COUNTRYSIDE DOES NOT ABOUND WITH GOTHIC REVIVAL HOUSES AS IT does with the Greek Revival. The Grant Knight House is one of the finest and best-preserved examples of the Gothic Revival style in this region of Kentucky.

James Knight was a Revolutionary War soldier who migrated to Kentucky in 1783 to claim a land grant in what is now Jessamine County. This property was called Homeplace, and a log house on now-adjoining land was most likely one of the early Knight structures. The Gothic Revival house was built by James Knight's son, Grant, probably about the mid-1800s, for Grant died in 1865 and is buried in a family graveyard on the property.

In his master's thesis, architectural historian Patrick A. Snadon says, "The Grant Knight House is a particularly fine wood Gothic cottage with triple gables across the front, and an outset entrance bay housing a central stair hall. Above the entrance is a triple window, in wood, much like that of Loudoun in stone, in Lexington. The house has double-bay windows at each end, and a pair of high double-brick chimney stacks linked at the top. There is some indication that a rear wing has been added to the T-shaped structure, but otherwise, it is little altered. The front porch is one of those graceful Carpenter's Gothic examples . . . consisting of octagonal posts, arches and trefoil tracery."

This wooden, horizontally-sided Gothic Revival cottage is an excellent example of those few remaining romantic structures in the Bluegrass. Its distinctive pointed dormers emphasize the verticality of this handsome country residence and reiterate the attempt by builders to break the traditions of the classical style that dominated the Bluegrass landscape for so many years.

The Grant Knight House

KEENE SPRINGS HOTEL

THERE PROBABLY ISN'T ANOTHER BUILDING IN KENTUCKY THAT BETTER REPRESENTS THE summer resorts that flourished in the mid-nineteenth century than the Keene Springs Hotel. According to historian J. Winston Coleman in his *Old Kentucky Watering Places*,

> Visits to the Kentucky watering places marked a period of festivities, looked forward to by both young and old, "when love making, electioneering, fighting, racing and general jollification reigned." Dr. J. J. Moorman, noted authority on the health resorts of the South, said of those in Kentucky: "Here night and day are passed in a round of eating and drinking, bathing and fiddling, dancing and reveling. Gaming is carried to a great excess and horse-racing is a daily amusement." . . . By the middle eighteen-forties the watering places of the state were in their heyday. All were flourishing and their proprietors vied with each other in the profusion of food, delicacy of viands, and perfection of service, as well as in extensiveness of accommodations and entertainment.

During this heyday period of the 1840s, white sulphur springs were discovered in the small village of Keene in Jessamine County. The present north end of the old frame hotel was moved to its site in 1843. It was soon enlarged by a long framed section connected to the log portion still standing at the south end of the hotel. The long middle section has regular, identical openings and, cantilevered from the second story, a decorative ninety-six-foot iron balcony. Guest rooms had openings out onto this and a rear balcony. The Jessamine County Survey states that "the Greek Revival styling of the hotel places it firmly within the resort hotel tradition of early and middle nineteenth century America."

In 1867, the Keene Springs Hotel was sold to the family of the present owner. It eventually became the general store of Keene, which was operated there until the present generation of the Wilson family built a new facility across the road. Today, the north end of the old hotel is used as a residence while the rest of the space is used for storage. Although the fashion for Kentucky spas waned before the turn of the century, the quaint Keene Springs Hotel building reminds us of the days when Kentuckians joined their brothers from the deeper South to "take the waters" of the many early Kentucky resorts.

Keene Springs Hotel

CHAUMIERE DES PRAIRIES

AT AGE 52, COLONEL DAVID MEADE, A PROMINENT TIDEWATER, VIRGINIA, PLANTER, came into what is now Jessamine County in the late eighteenth century and built what some consider the first "lordly estate" in Kentucky. The complex of buildings was widely acclaimed throughout this country and in Europe. There are several written accounts, a site plan, and a painting that reflect Chaumiere during the lifetime of Colonel Meade, but the only remaining structure is the octagonal brick wing now attached to a handsome, ca. 1840 Greek Revival house.

David Meade was born in 1744, the son of David and Susannah Everard Meade. Meade's father owned a handsome estate at the mouth of the Nansemond River in Virginia. At the age of seven, young David was sent to England, where he attended Harrow School for ten years. He returned to Virginia, married, and led the life of an aristocratic Virginian. Selling the ancestral home, he bought his own etate, which he called Maycox, on the James River, and here he practiced the fine art of landscape gardening and entertained the gentry of the Old Dominion.

There is no evidence to explain why Colonel Meade left his Virginia home in the prime of his life, but he and his family migrated into the wilderness of Kentucky in 1796 to settle on 300 acres he had purchased the year before. In this wilderness, he established a gracious lifestyle, which must have contributed to the transformation of the Bluegrass region from a rough frontier into a social and cultural center.

There are many personal accounts by those who visited Chaumiere, describing at length the Meades' way of life and their beautiful gardens. Their guests at various times included James Monroe, Andrew Jackson, Henry Clay, and Zachary Taylor. According to tradition, the surviving octagonal room was built in 1823 in anticipation of a visit by Lafayette, which, however, did not take place.

In 1838, the farm was purchased by Edward Carter, who constructed this handsome two-story house, built onto the only remaining part of Chaumiere. This generously-scaled Greek Revival house attracts considerable interest in its unusual, asymmetrical plan and the recessed entry patterned after Minard Lafever designs. Still known as Chaumiere des Prairies—Cottage in the Meadows—this fine house, with its remnant of the days when Colonel Meade presided here as the ultimate country gentleman, is well tended by the grand-daughter of the man who purchased Chaumiere in 1884.

Chaumiere Des Prairies

WAVELAND

SITUATED NEAR THE JESSAMINE-FAYETTE COUNTY LINE, THIS HOUSE, ORIGINALLY known as Providence, was constructed on a hill at the headwater of South Elkhorn Creek.

The house, built ca. 1840 for Craig Ashurst, is described in *Survey of Historic Sites in Kentucky — Jessamine County* as follows: "This brick Greek-Revival house follows the most popular format for Greek houses — two-story main block with a somewhat lower two-story ell with a recessed gallery of brick piers. All windows of the main facade are triple, and the central doorway and portico constitute a decorative assembly of fluted pilasters and Ionic columns. The cornice of both portico and main block are elaborated with dentils." The Tyrone limestone foundation was quarried from an outcropping of this stone several hundred feet from the site of the house.

Craig Ashurst had married Sallie Cravens in 1826, and his name first appears on the Jessamine County tax lists in 1833 as the owner of 174 acres on "Alcorn" watercourse. "Alcorn" should have been Elkhorn, the correct name for the creek by which he assembled land for a sizeable farm. The Ashurst family had been among the early settlers in the Bluegrass region. Craig Ashurst's mother, Jane Craig, was the daughter of Joseph Craig, one of the founders of the "Travelling Church," whose whole congregation left Orange County, Virginia, to settle together in Kentucky. The builder's daughter, Nannie Ashurst, married Massie Bryant, the great-great-nephew of Daniel Boone, and it was at Providence that they made their home.

In 1897, the Bryants sold their farm, and today it remains in the family that purchased it, with the fourth generation in residence. It was in this century and by this family that the house was called Waveland, for from its hilltop site one enjoys the rolling Bluegrass land set with century-old trees.

Waveland

Parlor

GLOSSARY

Arcade: a series of arches, resting on piers or columns.

Architrave: the lowest horizontal member of an entablature.

Archivolt: the inner molding around an arch, corresponding to the straight architrave in an entablature.

Bargeboard or vergeboard: the vertical-face board following, and set back under, the roof edge of a gable, sometimes decorated by carving.

Bay: one of several vertical divisions of a building usually marked by openings. For example, a five-bay house is one with five openings located on the front facade.

Belt course: projecting courses of stretcher bricks, usually found on the front facade of a house between the first and second stories.

Bracket: a projecting decorative element often in the form of a scroll, beneath an overhang; usually seen supporting the overhang of a roof.

Carpenter lock: usually a square metal lock that projects from the interior face of the door.

Chairrail: a molding around a room to prevent chairs, when pushed back against the wall, from damaging the surface of the wall.

Chamfered post: one where the edges, usually at the lower part, have been cut away as a decorative element.

Common bond: a type of brickwork composed of several rows laid on their long side (stretchers) with an occasional row laid with the short ends (headers) exposed.

Consoles: decorative brackets, usually with a scroll shape at its top and bottom.

Corinthian: the Greek order in which the column is distinguished by the capital usually being ornamented with an acanthus leaf motif.

Crenellation: alternating depressions resembling castle battlements above the roofline.

Crossetted architrave: the ends of the architrave (the horizontal piece resting on columns), which are extended to form a shape commonly called a "Greek ear"; most often found on Greek Revival door and window frames.

Dentil: one of a series of block-like projections, resembling teeth, forming a molding.

Distyle in antis: two columns supporting the upper wall in a doorway recess.

Dogtrot: a covered passage or breezeway joining two parts of a house; most commonly seen in log structures.

Doric: the Greek order in which the column is distinguished by having no base and an unornamented capital.

Double-pile: a double-pile house is one which is two rooms deep.

Eastlake: ornamentation on houses, popular during the Victorian period; named after Charles Eastlake, an English furniture designer. This style is most noted for its turned spindlework.

Elliptical: as used with arch, fanlight or window; one which is in the shape of a half-circle or half-oval.

Entablature: the horizontal part of a classical order resting on the columns or pilasters; it has three parts—the architrave, the frieze, and, on top, the cornice.

Fanlight: a window over a door either half-circular or half-elliptical in shape.

Federal: early nineteenth-century architectural style.

Flemish bond: brickwork laid in a pattern that alternates the long side of the brick (stretcher) and the end of the brick (header).

Frieze: the middle part of an entablature, sometimes containing relief carvings.

Gable roof: a sloping roof that forms a triangle shape at its ends.

Gallery: a long narrow room or covered porch.

Gambrel roof: a roof with two slopes of different pitch on either side of the ridge; in America, most common on "Dutch Colonial" style houses.

Gothic Revival: mid-nineteenth-century style in America, inspired by the European Gothic; some distinguishing features are gables with decorative bargeboards and windows with pointed-arch shape.

Gouge work: incised woodwork for which the gouge is the principal tool; seen most often in early mantel decoration.

Greek Revival: dominant style of American domestic architecture from about 1830 to the 1860s; inspired by ancient Greek buildings.

Hall-and-parlor plan: two front spaces of a house, one being the hall usually containing the staircase with a parlor flanking it.

Hipped roof: a roof that has four slopes instead of the two slopes of the ordinary gabled roof.

Hood mold: a protruding molding over a door or window to shed rainwater and as a decorative element; most commonly used on Italianate style buildings.

Ionic: the Greek order in which the column is distinguished by the form of the capital, which has a spiral scroll on either side.

Italianate: popular architectural style in America in the mid-nineteenth century, inspired by informal country Italian farmhouses.

Jack arch: most commonly a flat arch above a window or door usually formed by vertically-laid bricks.

Keystone: the wedge-shaped top member of an arch.

Lintel: the horizontal member over an opening in a wall or over two or more pillars or posts.

Loggia: an enclosed gallery with a series of columns on one or both sides.

Lunette: an arched topped window.

Medallions: most frequently a circular or oval bas-relief used in decoration; usually centered in the ceiling, and from which chandeliers were often hung.

Quoins: the dressed decorative stones at the corners of buildings, usually projecting and alternating large and small.

Palladian window: a window with three connecting sections, the center one being arched.

Pavilion: a name sometimes given to a projecting wing at the flank of a building.

Pegged: as in windows and door frames, when frames are held together with wooden pegs; commonly used before the use of nails.

Pilaster: a flat-faced shallow representation of a column applied to a wall, with a base, shaft, and capital.

Portico: a large columned porch.

Sash: the unit of a window that raises and lowers and contains the glass.

Second Empire: dominant architectural style for American buildings between the 1860s and the 1880s, the principal features of which were the mansard roof with dormer windows and decorative brackets beneath the eaves.

Stringer: the decorative end along the outer face of a flight of stairs.

Tetrastyle (Tetra-style): classical style having four columns on a portico.

Transom: an opening or window over a door or a window.

Tudor style: building that exhibt architectural detailings that mimic the architectural characteristics of Tudor (early sixteenth-century) England. Some distinguishing features are exposed half-timbering, massive chimneys, and narrow windows.

Tuscan: the Roman order in which the column is slender and has a base and plain shaft.

Water table: an offset of rounded, molded bricks occurring on the external base of a wall.